DON'T PANIC

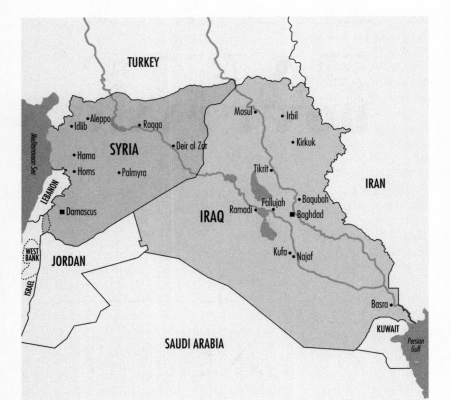

DON'T PANIC

ISIS, TERROR AND TODAY'S MIDDLE EAST

GWYNNE DYER

RANDOM HOUSE CANADA

PUBLISHED BY RANDOM HOUSE CANADA

Copyright © 2015 Gwynne Dyer

All rights reserved under International and Pan-American Copyright
Conventions. No part of this book may be reproduced in any form or by any
electronic or mechanical means, including information storage and retrieval
systems, without permission in writing from the publisher, except by a reviewer,
who may quote brief passages in a review. Published in 2015 by Random House
Canada, a division of Penguin Random House Canada Limited. Distributed in
Canada by Penguin Random House Canada Limited, Toronto.

www.penguinrandomhouse.ca

Library and Archives Canada Cataloguing in Publication

Dyer, Gwynne, author
    Don't panic : ISIS, terror and today's Middle East / Gwynne Dyer.

Issued in print and electronic formats.

ISBN 978-0-345-81586-6
eBook ISBN 978-0-345-81587-3

    1. IS (Organization). 2. Terrorism—Middle East. 3. Terrorism—
Religious aspects—Islam. 4. Middle East—History—21st century. I. Title.

HV6431.D93 2015   956.05'4   C2015-902702-0

Book design by Andrew Roberts
Cover image: © Medyan Dairieh / ZUMA Press/ Corbis
Map designed by Adrian So

Printed and bound in the United States of America

10 9 8 7 6 5 4 3 2 1

Penguin
Random House
RANDOM HOUSE CANADA

CONTENTS

———————•———————

INTRODUCTION

Far too much is written about terrorism. Even worse, most of it is sensationalist claptrap, which means there is a constant need to deflate the bubble of fabricated fear and restore some kind of perspective. Somebody has to do it, and maybe it's my turn.

What makes me particularly reluctant to wade into the subject of terrorism again is that it means discussing a lot of foolish, fanatical or just plain evil people who are also Muslims. After a while you start to feel that no matter how many times you say that Islamist terrorists and those who support them are only a small minority of the world's Muslims—certainly a smaller minority than the proportion of Irish Catholics who supported the IRA, or Sri Lankan Tamils who supported the Tamil Tigers— you still wind up sounding like you are saying that Muslims are the problem. On the other hand, three of the four terrorist incidents I was personally witness to (Bombay 1993, Moscow 2001, London 2007) *did* involve bombs set by Muslim terrorists. In the past decade and a half, the great majority of the terrorist attacks in the world were carried out by Muslims, so how can we not discuss it?

Al Qaeda is out, and ISIS is in. The latter's executions are more dramatic, and they make better videos: the one of the Jordanian fighter pilot being burned alive in an iron cage was shot simultaneously from seven different camera angles. ISIS attracts more lost young men and women from the Muslim diaspora in the West than stuffy old al Qaeda: there are practically line-ups at the Turkish-Syrian border. And now they even have their own "Islamic State," with its own flag and a caliph and everything. Let's have a book about that.

Well, okay, but I don't want to scare people. They are far too frightened already, because the actual threat is very small unless you happen to live in one of the worst-affected countries of the Middle East. It is the media-fuelled fear gripping people in the West that empowers and indeed compels Western governments to do reckless things that actually serve the terrorists' agenda. No surprise in that: these hair-trigger responses are precisely what today's terrorism is designed to produce. That's why I call this book *DON'T PANIC* (with humble thanks to Douglas Adams).[1]

On the other hand, we have to take the terrorists seriously. That's not to say that we must take them at their own valuation; they are considerably less important than they think they are. But ISIS, al Qaeda, al Nusra, Boko Haram, al Shabaab and the rest are revolutionaries with a political programme, not just vicious idiots with guns. Their political programme, for those who do not share their own very particular religious convictions, starts at the implausible and ends up deep into the surreal, but all their actions, even the sickest and most cruel, are calculated to bring the day nearer when that programme will be fulfilled.

A lot of the foot soldiers in any army haven't the slightest idea what the strategy is, or any interest in learning about it. All that the men with the box-cutters on the hijacked flights of 9/11 needed to know was that they were going to be "martyred" and go straight to paradise. They neither knew nor much cared what strategic benefits for the cause Osama bin Laden expected to gain from the massacre they were about to commit. But the people who make the plans and choose the targets are not only competent strategists; they are also good psychologists, for terrorism succeeds mainly through the perceptions it creates, not the actual damage it does. Being wicked does not make you stupid—more's the pity.

So this book will have to do a number of things, if I get it right. First, it will explain why the Muslim world, and in particular the Arab world, has become the global capital of terrorism (the great majority of the victims being Muslims themselves, and in particular Arabs). Second, it will explain how terrorism works, by which I mean how it often (not always) brings those who employ its tactics closer to their expressed goals. Third, it will trace the evolution of terrorist strategies and terrorist organizations in the Arab world, for they have both mutated over time. Finally, it will offer some thoughts on what we ought to be doing about the "terrorist threat."

I will be treating these four themes in parallel, or even all at once, because this is a story that has unfolded over more than thirty years and I would distort matters too greatly if I told it thematically rather than in sequence. Experts will spot places where I am eliding some of the finer detail of the story in the interest of concision, but I have tried not to leave out anything important.

The past dozen years, since the misbegotten U.S. invasion of Iraq in 2003, have seen an almost continuous growth in the scale and reach of the Islamist revolutionary groups in the Arab world. In 2013 the Global Terrorism Index recorded 17,958 deaths, a 60 percent jump in just one year and a fivefold increase since 2000. Eighty percent of those deaths occurred in only five countries—Iraq, Afghanistan, Pakistan, Nigeria and Syria—and almost all of the victims were Muslims. So were the groups that did most of the killing: Islamic State in Iraq and Syria, Boko Haram in Nigeria, the Taliban in Afghanistan, the various franchises of al Qaeda, and the assorted Islamist groups in Pakistan. The Islamists are definitely on a roll now, and we will probably see more seizures of territory in out-of-the-way parts of the Arab countries and in Muslim-majority regions of the adjacent African countries, followed in all likelihood by further pledges of allegiance to the "Islamic caliphate," whose seat, as of the summer of 2015, is in Raqqa in eastern Syria.

But this rapid territorial expansion has been accompanied by a slide in the dominant Islamist ideology, away from the patient, pragmatic and flexible style of al Qaeda towards the intoxicating "End-Times" eschatology of ISIS. History as they see it now has a script, and the duty of those who serve Islamic State is to bring about the Apocalypse, all the way from the great battle at Dabiq (a town in northern Syria) that starts the sequence running down to the Last Battle at Jerusalem, where Isa—Jesus, to Christians—spears the anti-messiah, Dajjal, and then the world ends.

You would certainly not like to see such people in charge of a powerful modern state, but that is unlikely precisely because they are that kind of people. Bin Laden wanted to achieve such a state, spanning first the whole Arab world, then the entire Muslim world, and ultimately the whole world, and he was prepared to take any path that opened up, for however long it took, to reach his goal. The ISIS lot just want to live out the apocalyptic script in the shorter term. Which does help the situation a bit, because they cannot deviate from the script. We know where they want to go.

One last thing. The Muslim world, or at least its Middle Eastern heartland, now stands on the brink of a sectarian confrontation between Sunnis and Shias that is potentially as big, as long and as violent as the religious wars between Catholics and Protestants in sixteenth- and seventeenth-century Europe. This looming threat is often portrayed, especially in the Western media, as an inevitable clash between two groups of fanatics, but it is nothing of the sort.

No reputable historian would explain Europe's religious wars as merely a matter of rival religious doctrines. They were intensely political events, in which sectarian loyalties were ruthlessly manipulated in the service of domestic and foreign political goals. The same goes for the Middle East today—and the right question to ask is: why now?

There's an obvious explanation for why the Christian religious wars happened when they did: they were triggered by the second great schism in Christianity, which involved all of Western and Central Europe. It's less obvious why Sunnis and Shias should be at each others' throats right now, given that the schism between the two main branches of Islam happened thirteen centuries ago. There were many bloody clashes between them at that time, but in most subsequent generations, in places where the population was mixed, ordinary Sunnis and Shias lived in peace. In modern secular states like pre-invasion Iraq, even intermarriages between the two communities were commonplace.

Moreover, nine out of ten Muslims are Sunni. You can imagine that this might lead to an occasional massacre of Shias, but certainly not to a stand-up fight. However, in the Middle East the Sunni-Shia ratio is much less lopsided. In the space between Egypt and Iran, Sunnis have a two-thirds overall majority, but the country-by-country ratios range from 85 percent Shia in Iran to 90 percent Sunni in Egypt. And in the countries bordering on the Gulf—Iran, Iraq, Saudi Arabia and the smaller Gulf kingdoms and emirates—Shias have an overall majority of at least a two-to-one, due mainly to the very big population of Iran.

(This large body of water used to be known in English as the Persian Gulf, but that annoys Arabs so much that tactful people now say simply "The Gulf".)

The trigger for the current Sunni-Shia confrontation was the 1979 revolution in Iran, which became an "Islamic Republic" ruled to a large extent by Shia clerics. The overthrow of the Shah and Iran's successful defiance of the West made the Iranian revolution very popular among Arabs, even Sunni Arabs, who were living under dictators and absolute monarchs who were for the most part in thrall to the West. The alarmed rulers of some Arab countries, especially those in the Arabian peninsula, sought to counter this trend by emphasizing that Shia are heretics deserving punishment (from a Sunni point of view), and in this enterprise they were greatly aided by the tens of billions of dollars that Saudi Arabia has spent in spreading its particular version of Sunni Islam, Wahhabism, throughout the Arab world (and the broader Muslim world as well). Wahhabism has been virulently anti-Shia ever since its emergence in northern Saudi Arabia in the eighteenth century.

If we were talking about Christian sects, we would classify Wahhabism as fundamentalist. It is deeply conservative, even to the point of retaining traditional punishments like beheading and stoning that had largely disappeared in other parts of the Muslim world. It is very concerned with ridding Islam of what it sees as later distortions of the original faith and getting back to the values that it believes were embodied in the lives of the first generations after the death of the Prophet Muhammad. This fundamentalism naturally intensifies the Wahhabis' hostility towards the Shias, whose split with the Sunnis dates from the first generation after the death of Muhammad in the seventh century.

Wahhabi leaders have been closely allied with the Saudi ruling house since 1744, and Saudi Arabia's enormous wealth now gives their ideas great influence in Muslim communities everywhere, even among people who would not describe themselves as Wahhabis. A 2012 study by Pew Research, a non-partisan "fact tank," revealed that 40 percent of Sunni Palestinians, 50 percent of Sunni Moroccans, and 53 percent of Sunni Egyptians now say that Shias are not Muslims. No opinion polls were done on this topic fifty years ago, but a mass of circumstantial evidence indicates that as recently as the 1960s such extreme views were very rare among Sunnis.

Other varieties of Sunni believers who will crop up in this book are Salafis and takfiris. The Salafis share the basic Wahhabi conviction that it is necessary to get back to the early values of Islam, and are similarly puritanical and literalist in their approach to religion—indeed, some Wahhabis actually prefer to be called Salafis—but they do not have ties with the house of Saud. Some are militant and willing to use violence to further their cause; others work peacefully towards the same goals. Takfiris also espouse the basic Wahhabi beliefs, but are distinguished by their conviction that any Muslim who does not share

them is an "apostate" whom it is lawful and even neces-
sary to kill. They also believe quite strongly in the need to
kill Shias and expunge this great heresy from the planet.
They are not exactly a sect, but it is they who populate the
Sunni extremist movements now fighting to overthrow
Shia-dominated governments in Syria and Iraq.

On the Shia side there are also various sects with different beliefs, though none as extreme as the Sunni takfiris.
The Alawites, who dominate the regime of Bashar al Assad
in Syria, are a divergent and secretive sect of Shia Islam
that incorporates elements of Christianity and other religions, and is seen even by some other Shias as not really
Muslim. Another group sometimes mistakenly seen as an
even more divergent Shia sect are the Druze, who also live
mostly in Syria. However, their faith, while it is a mono-
theistic religion largely in the Abrahamic tradition, incorporates elements of Jewish, Christian, Muslim, and even
Hindu and Buddhist beliefs, and they do not see themselves as Muslims.

Sorry that took so long, but you really can't tell the players
without a programme.

CHAPTER 1

TO UNDERSTAND ALL
IS NOT TO
FORGIVE ALL . . .

but it does help to predict the terrorists' actions and respond intelligently. Unfortunately, the West has been spectacularly bad at doing that.

We will conduct a systematic campaign of air strikes against these terrorists.

– U.S. president Barack Obama on ISIS, 2014

This is about psychopathic terrorists who are trying to kill us. Like it or not they have already declared war on us.
[So bomb them in Iraq.]

– U.K. prime minister David Cameron on bombing ISIS, London, 2014

We cannot stand on the sidelines while ISIL continues to promote terrorism in Canada as well as against our allies and partners, nor can we allow ISIL to have a safe haven in Syria.
[Bomb them in Syria too.]

– Canadian prime minister Stephen Harper, Ottawa, 2015

Bomb, bomb, bomb, bomb, bomb Iran . . .

– U.S. Senator John McCain during the 2008 presidential campaign[2]

To be fair, Senator McCain has not actually advocated bombing Iran for the past few years. He has been too busy advocating bombing Syria. At first he only wanted to bomb the regime's troops, but latterly he has urged the Obama administration to bomb *both* Syrian president Bashar al Assad's forces and the new "Islamic State" founded by ISIS on Syrian and Iraq territory. Why not? Two enemies for the price of one.

John McCain comes close to self-parody, but the distance between him and more "serious" Western leaders is not very great. Some of them (probably including Barack Obama) privately understand that bombing generally makes more new enemies for the West than it kills old ones, but domestic politics usually trumps foreign policy, and the domestic audience wants its leaders to "do something." Bombing people in the Middle East is something Western governments can do without incurring significant casualties on their own side, so it is politically safe and answers the public demand for action. More often than not the action ends up being counter-productive in foreign policy terms, but that is a lesser consideration.

A more serious approach would begin by trying to understand the motives, goals and strategies of the disparate terrorist groups that allegedly threaten us. That is not easy, because their perspectives on history, their political values, and their understanding of their religion are all quite unfamiliar to most people in the West. Indeed, parts of their belief system still seem pretty bizarre (if no longer unfamiliar) to a majority of mainstream Sunni Muslims as well. (Shia Muslims, by and large, do not indulge in terrorist attacks on Western targets.) To make matters more complicated, the Islamist terrorist groups have differing theological views and different specific goals, although they all have a lot in common.

In order to get a sense of just how complex the situation is, consider the range of attacks and initiatives by Islamist fighters between March 18 and April 3, 2015. (I chose this period simply because that's when I was writing this chapter.)

March 18: Two young Tunisians who had crossed the border into Libya for weapons training return home and attack cruise-ship tourists visiting the Bardo Museum in Tunis. Twenty-two people are killed, all but three of them foreign tourists, before the terrorists run out of bullets and are killed by Tunisian police. ISIS claims responsibility for the attack two days later, saying it was a "blessed invasion of one of the dens of infidels and vice in Muslim Tunisia."

March 22: ISIS in Yemen sends four suicide bombers to attack two Shia mosques in Sana'a, killing 137 people. Houthi (Shia) rebels from the north, having already taken central Yemen, including the capital, push south to drive the incumbent government from its last stronghold, Aden. Fighters from AQAP (Al Qaeda in the Arabian Peninsula) also approach Aden from the east, causing U.S. Special Operations troops who controlled drone strikes in the region to blow up their heavy equipment at a nearby airbase and flee across the Red Sea to Djibouti. Now no American troops remain in Yemen.

March 25: Libya's Tobruk-based government-in-exile announces an offensive to retake the city of Derna from ISIS and other militant groups. It presumably fails, as nothing further is heard about it.

March 26: Saudi Arabia, convinced that the Houthi rebels in Yemen are controlled by Shia Iran, creates a coalition that includes most Sunni-ruled Arab countries (Saudi Arabia, Egypt, Sudan, Jordan, Kuwait, Bahrain, Qatar, the United Arab Emirates and Morocco) plus Pakistan, and begins bombing targets across the whole of Houthi-controlled Yemen. A ground invasion by Egyptian, Saudi and Pakistani troops will follow, the Saudis announce, if deemed necessary.

March 27: Syrian rebel forces dominated by the al Qaeda-linked Nusra Front capture Idlib, only the second Syrian provincial capital to fall in almost four years of war.

March 28–29: Boko Haram gunmen kill at least forty-three voters during the Nigerian national elections. Earlier in the month, Boko Haram's leader, Abubakar Shekau, formally declared his organization's allegiance to Islamic State, the ISIS-run "caliphate" in eastern Syria and western Iraq.

March 31: ISIS rebels gain control of much of the Palestinian refugee camp of Yarmouk, a southern suburb of Damascus. It is the first foothold of ISIS forces in the Syrian capital.

April 2: Al Shabaab gunmen from Somalia make a pre-dawn attack on Garissa University College in northeastern Kenya (near the Somali border) and kill 148 people, the overwhelming majority of them students. The students are asked their religion and Christians are killed at once, while Muslims are spared. Kenyan authorities say the attack was organized by Mohamed Mohamud, a Somali-speaking Kenyan citizen who was a lecturer at the college.

April 2: Attacks on army checkpoints by Islamist militants of the Ansar Beit al Maqdis group in Egypt's northern Sinai region kill ten soldiers and two civilians. In November 2014, the group had declared its allegiance to Islamic State: "In accordance with the teachings of the Prophet, we announce our allegiance to the Caliphate, and call on Muslims everywhere to do the same."

April 2: Al Qaeda in the Arabian Peninsula forces seize the port city of Mukalla and the largest army base in eastern Yemen, effectively establishing AQAP control over the sparsely populated eastern half of the country.

April 3: The Iraqi government announces that it has recaptured the almost entirely Sunni city of Tikrit, the first significant loss of territory by ISIS since it overran western and northwestern Iraq in July 2014. But it takes Iraqi government forces almost a month to retake the city, and the fighting is done mostly by Shia militias, not by the Iraqi regular army (which collapsed during the ISIS offensive in 2014 and still has only a few units that are fit for combat).

The Shia militias celebrate their victory by lynching not only captured ISIS fighters but also some of the few Sunni civilians who had stayed in their homes (on the grounds that they must have been ISIS supporters if they hadn't fled). They also loot and burn hundreds of businesses and private homes. On April 4 Iraq finally pulls the militiamen out of the city, but the damage has been done: their behaviour will produce even more Sunni recruits for ISIS forces in the rest of the Iraqi territory controlled by Islamic State, and make its recapture even more difficult.

Confronted with all these complex alliances, bitter hatreds and inherited obsessions, and bewildered by all this churning violence, the average outsider is tempted to decide they're all crazy and just ignore the whole mess. That could even be the best thing to do in some cases, but the problem is that at least some of the violence will affect the West no matter what it does or doesn't do. So it's worth trying to understand what's actually going on and why.

Take the sixteen days of atrocities listed above, for example. At first glance it seems that almost half of the victims enumerated were non-Muslims, but that is an optical illusion. We know the actual numbers of dead in the Tunisian and Kenyan attacks, but comparable killings in Syria, Iraq and Yemen were not enumerated, because innocent civilian dead are rarely counted accurately (or even at all) in that kind of fighting. Even excluding those who died in combat or were part of the "collateral damage," and counting only those who were deliberately executed for being the wrong kind of Muslim, the Muslim death toll during that period would certainly be at least a low multiple of the non-Muslim victims of terrorism.

The slaughter at the Bardo Museum in Tunisia (March 18) was intended to advance the cause of Islamist revolution in a Muslim country. The victims were foreign tourists, and Tunisia depends on tourism for about 10 percent of its Gross Domestic Product and an even higher proportion of its jobs. The Bardo attack frightened many tourists away, and the subsequent slaughter of 38 foreign tourists by a lone terrorist on Sousse beach on June 26 pretty well closed Tunisia's tourism industry down, so most of those jobs will now vanish. This may destabilize the country, which is a high priority for Islamist revolutionaries, because the country was home to the sole successful non-violent democratic revolution of the Arab Spring. For the Islamists' project to succeed there, they need to discredit and destroy the reforms of that revolution.

The fighting in Yemen (March 22, March 26 and April 2) began as just one more of the tribal power struggles that litter Yemeni history. The Houthis, who have had great success in the current civil war, are Shias (as are about two-fifths of the Yemeni population), but the war is not primarily about religion. At least as important is the fact that the Houthis are northerners in a country with a deep historical split between north and south. Moreover, they are allied with Yemen's former president, Ali Abdullah Saleh, who was forced to resign in 2012 under the terms of a "Gulf Initiative" that had strong Saudi Arabian support.

The air strikes and the threat of a land invasion by a Saudi-led pan-Arab alliance of Sunni countries are intended to stop the Houthis from taking control of Yemen because the Saudis, who see an Iranian plotter behind every bush, have convinced themselves that the Houthis are actually just a tool in an Iranian power play to establish a Shia base on Saudi Arabia's southern border. But in amongst all this paranoia and folly, two Islamist groups, al Qaeda in the Arabian Peninsula and ISIS, have set themselves up in the less populated south and east of the country with the intention of creating bases of their own. Indeed, they are doubtless hoping at this point that if the Saudi-led coalition breaks the Houthi hold on Yemen but does not get its own troops on the ground fast enough and in sufficient numbers, the Islamists will be able to sweep the board with their own fighters and create another branch of "Islamic State" like the existing one in Syria and Iraq. AQAP and ISIS would probably end up fighting each other for control of that state, but they may be capable of cooperating long enough to set it up, if they get the chance.

The Syrian civil war (March 27 and March 31) stumbles on, with advances by Islamist anti-regime forces both in the north and in the outskirts of the capital, Damascus. The point to note here is that all the non-Islamist forces have been either driven out of business or absorbed by the Islamists in the course of four years of fighting. The U.S. government, which still wants to believe it can avoid supporting either the Islamists or Bashar al Assad's blood-soaked dictatorship, continues to insist that it can build some "third force" of rebels who will defeat both the regime and the Islamists, but that is sheer fantasy. Sooner or later Washington will have to choose.

Boko Haram (March 28–29) has had things all its own way for the past three years, mainly because the Nigerian army could not or would not fight, but the government was finally forced to focus on the insurgency in the northeast because of the upcoming general election (which had to be postponed), and the death toll during the voting was much lower than had been feared. The decision of Abubakar Shekau to affiliate his organization with Abu Bakr al Baghdadi's Islamic State is largely symbolic at this point, as little or no direct contact is possible between the two, but it does show the power of the idea: the territories controlled by the two men are 3,000 miles (5,000 kilometres) apart.

The massacre of Christians in northeastern Kenya (April 2), one of a number of massacres carried out by the Somali terrorist group al Shabaab in the past three years, is "retaliation" for the dispatch of Kenyan troops to Somalia as part of an African Union force. The force has the task of restoring peace in the country after a quarter century of anarchy and civil war, but in practice its main enemy has been al Shabaab, which has been part of the al Qaeda network for more than three years. (It had been asking to join since 2009, but Osama bin Laden rejected its application, urging it to review its operations "in order to minimize its toll to Muslims." This is probably why it now kills mainly Christians in its attacks in Kenya, but in Somalia itself the great majority of its victims are, of course, Muslims.)

The Ansar Beit al Maqdis group in Egypt (April 2) has not yet extended its operations to Cairo, where other Islamist terrorist groups have been active since the military overthrow of the elected Muslim Brotherhood government led by Mohamed Morsi in 2013. However, it does enjoy a fair degree of control over the northern Sinai coastal region, particularly in the area close to the Israeli frontier. In the ongoing competition between al Qaeda and Islamic State franchises, Ansar Beit al Maqdis has opted for the latter.

The atrocities in Iraq during the reconquest of Tikrit (March 3) were one more sign that the local power struggles in various Arab countries where Sunnis and Shias used to live side by side in relative peace (Lebanon, Syria, Iraq and the kingdoms and emirates of the Arabian peninsula) are beginning to coalesce into a generalized Sunni-Shia war. This would be a catastrophe that could blight the entire region for a generation.

One overriding conclusion is unavoidable: the people of the region, regardless of their specific political and sectarian loyalties, are very, *very* angry. Angry at their history, angry at those whom they hold responsible for their history, angry even at themselves for allowing themselves to become the victims of that vicious, lethal history.

They tell a story in the Middle East—if you've heard it before, stop me now—about a scorpion who wanted to cross a river. Being unable to swim, he asked a frog to carry him over on his back. The frog refused, fearing that the scorpion might sting him and kill him, but the scorpion pointed out that he would never do such a thing because if the frog died, he would drown. "Okay, hop on," said the frog, and set out across the river. Halfway across, the scorpion stung the frog. As they both sank beneath the water, the frog gasped out, "Why?" "This is the Middle East," the scorpion explained.

Among the educated Arab elite there is a pervasive historical melancholy about the lost Golden Age, the first four centuries after Arab armies overran the southern and eastern territories of the (by then Christian) Roman Empire in the latter 600s. As the Arab conquerors had the wit to retain and even improve upon the administrative and scientific accomplishments of the Greco-Roman cultures they now ruled, the early Arab empires were culturally, technologically and intellectually superior to any other civilization in western Eurasia except, perhaps, Byzantium (what was left of the Eastern Roman Empire after the conquests).

The tide began to turn with the real start of the Christian *reconquista* in al Andalus (Muslim-ruled Spain) in the mid-eleventh century, although it took four more centuries to extinguish Muslim rule in all of Spain and Portugal. Around the same time, the Arabic-speaking parts of the Levant (Palestine, Syria, Iraq) were conquered by the Seljuk Turks, an Islamized pastoral people from Central Asia who originally spoke Turkish but used Persian as an administrative language. By the time that the First Crusade, a Western European campaign to recapture the formerly Christian lands on the eastern shores of the Mediterranean, culminated in the Christian conquest of Jerusalem in 1099, the whole of the eastern Arab world was already under foreign rule. The resistance to the Crusaders was commanded mainly by Kurdish and Turkish leaders, not by Arabs.

The Crusades finally petered out in defeat with the fall of the last Christian stronghold in the Holy Land in 1291; but by then a far greater calamity had struck the Arab world: the Mongol destruction of Baghdad, and indeed of all of Iraq, in 1258. (Iraq did not recover to its pre-Mongol level of population until the early twentieth century.) The Arab Golden Age was over, and no genuinely Arab regime again ruled over the agricultural heartland of the Arab world, from Egypt to Iraq, until the latter part of the twentieth century. Indeed, from the early sixteenth century on it was all part of the Ottoman Empire, and its rulers spoke Turkish.

Arab intellectuals know every bitter step in this story of decline and defeat. The great majority of ordinary Arabs don't know the details of the story, of course, but they are well aware that something went terribly wrong in Arab history a long time ago, and that it has been downhill ever since. The last century is particularly bitter, and is well remembered by all parties. The Arabs were promised independence by the British during the First World War (Lawrence of Arabia and all that) and duly revolted against Ottoman rule, only to discover that Britain and France had made a secret deal in 1916 to carve up the Arab world between themselves. Under the Sykes-Picot Agreement, Britain got Iraq, Palestine and Jordan, and France got Syria and Lebanon (the British already had Egypt). Some Arabs refused to accept this carve-up, but their protests were crushed, and after 1918 there were once again no genuinely independent Arab countries except for a few impoverished sheikhdoms in the desert parts of Arabia.

After the Second World War ended in 1945 the European empires went into retreat, and during the 1950s and 1960s every Arab country got its independence (although some of them had to fight quite hard for it). The post-independence priority everywhere was not democracy but "modernization." These countries hungered desperately for prosperity and respect, and both seemed to be most readily attainable by following the Eastern European/Soviet model of rapid industrialization and educational uplift, which was doing quite well economically at the time. (Economic growth in

Soviet-bloc countries did not fall behind the capitalist/ democratic model until the later 1960s.) So a flock of young Arab military officers seized power from the kings and parliaments left behind by the departing imperial powers—Gamal Abdel Nasser in Egypt, Hafez al Assad in Syria, Muammar Gaddafi in Libya, and so on—promising to deliver a rapid rise in both national power and individual living standards. They also promised to put an end to the Israeli state, which had fought its way into existence in the very heart of the Arab world, with much Western support, in 1948.

The new leaders failed everywhere. They failed militarily, losing further wars to Israel in 1956, 1967 and 1973, mainly because they lacked the organizational ability to take advantage of their vastly superior numbers: in every war from 1956 onwards, the Israelis actually had more troops on the battlefield than their Arab opponents (plus, of course, strong support from Britain and France, and later from the United States as well). They failed economically because they were military officers whose training had not prepared them in any way to run countries and manage economies. And even if they had had the right skills, the development model they adopted, which in the end did not work that well even in the "socialist" countries of Eastern Europe, was hopelessly inappropriate for countries with low literacy, low urbanization, almost no industrial or scientific establishment, strong tribal and clan identities, and deeply rooted patriarchal values. At any rate, they failed, and by the late 1970s it was clear to everybody that they had failed.

A six-paragraph tale of woe spanning almost a millennium, but it does explain why Arabs are so angry. They feel cheated by the West, by their own governments, by history. Even today there is little modern industry and almost no serious scientific research happening in the Arab countries. Average incomes (except in the few oil-rich states) are lower than in any other region of the world except sub-Saharan Africa—and on current trend lines will fall even below Africa's in another ten or fifteen years. Half the women in the Arab world are illiterate.

As for the military rulers who had presided over this full-spectrum failure, they did not retire from power in disgrace; they clung fiercely to power despite their failures, and as their popularity declined their regimes compensated by becoming more brutally oppressive. And they (or their lineages) survived a very long time: Gaddafi lasted forty-two years, Bashar al Assad is still in power forty-five years after his father took power in Syria, and General Abdel Fattah al Sisi is the fourth general to rule Egypt in unbroken succession (apart from the brief democratic experiment in 2011–13) since 1954. The surviving monarchies, like Morocco, Jordan and Saudi Arabia, have likewise changed little over the decades.

And so, naturally enough, many young Arabs who came to adulthood in the 1970s, trapped in the dead end of the generals' failed "modernization" projects, were driven to consider revolution as a way out. But a revolution needs an ideology, and in practice will not thrive if the ideology on offer is simply a warmed-over version of the one the revolutionaries are seeking to overthrow—"We will carry out the same modernization project, based on Soviet-style crash industrialization, but we will do it more efficiently than the lot currently in power." A completely different approach was needed, and many of the revolutionaries found it in the "Islamist" thought of an Egyptian writer, scholar and poet called Sayyid Qutb.

Qutb, born in a small village in upper Egypt in 1906, worked in Cairo as a senior official in the ministry of education but was also a successful literary figure who moved in high political and intellectual circles. Like many Egyptian men of his generation, he held deeply conservative social views, but there was nothing radical about him until he went on a two-and-a-half-year study tour in the United States in 1948–51 to study American educational methods. There he observed and was appalled by American ways, decided that he hated "Western civilization," and committed himself fully to an austere and fundamentalist version of Islam. He described churches as "entertainment centres and sexual playgrounds" and was particularly dismayed by the freedoms enjoyed by American women, writing that: "The American girl is well acquainted with her body's seductive capacity. She knows it lies in the face, and in expressive eyes, and thirsty lips. She knows seductiveness lies in the round breasts, the full buttocks, and in the shapely thighs, sleek legs—and she shows all this and does not hide it." (It need hardly be mentioned that Qutb never married because he could not find a woman of sufficient "moral purity and discretion.")[3]

On his return to Egypt Qutb quit the civil service and joined the Muslim Brotherhood, an organization that was itself then turning from peaceful agitation to violence, and became the chief of its propaganda section. In 1952 he began writing his eight-volume work, *In the Shadow of the Qur'an*. It was a strongly fundamentalist commentary on the holy book that emphasized the institution of jihad and depicted Jews, Christians and even those Muslims who did not fully obey the rules of Shari'ah (Islamic religious law)—including almost all of the dictators and kings who ruled the Arab countries but failed to impose Shari'ah law—as enemies of God. Qutb had no explicit views on what form of governance should follow once the rulers were overthrown—he has even been accused of "anarcho-Islamism"—but he was definitely anti-nationalist. There was only one Umma (the community of Muslim believers), and it must not be divided by national borders.

Where the military rulers and conservative monarchs of the Arab world peddled the fading vision of powerful Arab national states on the European model (but still Muslim, of course), Sayyid Qutb offered a return to the glorious Golden Age of the undivided caliphate. The revived caliphate would be very powerful too, of course—indeed, one day it would encompass the whole world—but he was largely silent on the physical sources of its power. Would it be heavily industrialized, urbanized, organized for efficient production? He didn't say, but one gets the impression that he thought not. Would it be democratic? Certainly not: it would function in accordance with God's laws as interpreted by Islamic scholars, not in response to the whims of mere men.

For many young Arabs who were deeply disillusioned by the failures of the existing order, it was an entrancing vision, but to those then in power it was clearly a mortal threat, and they responded accordingly. In 1954 Nasser ordered the arrest of Qutb and many other members of the Muslim Brotherhood. Qutb spent the next ten years in prison but after a few years was allowed to resume writing, and he managed to finish *In the Shadow of the Qur'an*. He was released in 1964, but rearrested in 1965 after an assassination attempt against Nasser by members of the Muslim Brotherhood. During his time at liberty he wrote his Islamist manifesto, *Milestones*, which argued that the corrupt, Westernized regimes of the Muslim world had to be overthrown in order for the world's Muslims to live as God intended. This policy could actually make it a religious duty for true Muslims to kill their "apostate" rulers and those who support them, a proposition that he defended in his last trial and which was used to justify his death sentence. He was not directly involved in the plot to kill Nasser, but he was tortured, given a show trial, and hanged in August 1966.

There were other prominent philosophers of the nascent Islamist movement like Rashid Rida, Hassan al-Banna and Maulana Mawdudi, but Sayyid Qutb was the most influential and the one most willing, despite his own rather meek and shy persona, to espouse and justify the use of violence in the construction of an Islamic state (or, as it is now called, "Islamic State"). After his death, his brother Muhammad Qutb moved to Saudi Arabia, where he became a professor of Islamic Studies at King Abdulaziz University and did much to publish and promote Sayyid Qutb's work. It is reported by a college friend of Osama bin Laden's that the founder of al Qaeda regularly attended Muhammad Qutb's weekly public lectures and read Sayyid Qutb's works.

So there you have it: why it is Arabs and not Indonesians or Turks or other Muslims who carry out most of terrorist attacks; why many Arabs are so very cross—and how a few Arab intellectuals rationalized not only the turn to violence but the killing of fellow Sunni Muslims. (Sayyid Qutb and his colleagues didn't actually work out justifications for killing Shia Muslims, because there were virtually no Shias in positions of power in Egypt and the nearby Arab countries they were mostly concerned with, but that was easily done when it became tactically desirable to start killing Shias.)

CHAPTER 2

———————•———————

IT'S NOT ALWAYS
ABOUT YOU

War is merely the continuation of politics by other means.

– Carl von Clausewitz, On War, 1832

S o is terrorism.

The enduring delusion that distorts and ulti-mately dooms Western responses to Islamist ter-rorism is the belief that the West is the main and most important target of Islamist attacks. Amidst such igno-rance, absurd conclusions like George W. Bush's explana-tion for 9/11—"they hate our values"—can sound plausible and even convincing to the general Western public. Islamist terrorists do regard Western "values" as sinful, by and large, but they are not in the business of reforming the West. Their focus is on gaining power in their own coun-tries. A complex paramilitary operation like 9/11 is a major undertaking for an Islamist revolutionary group like al Qaeda, and Osama bin Laden's people needed a concrete return on their investment of time, money and manpower. They got it. When Western armies plunged into the Middle East to "fight terrorism," the initial al Qaeda investment (nineteen men, some flying lessons, a few box-cutters) was repaid a thousandfold. So it would help a great deal if we could finally get it through our thick heads that it is not always about us.

Military strategy is a means to an end, not the end itself. Terrorism has its own strategies, and they too are means to an end. In the case of terrorism, the ultimate goal is usually revolution, and those being attacked are often members or supporters of the regime the revolutionaries wish to overthrow. But not always. Sometimes, the revolutionaries will direct their terrorism at third parties, in the hope that those outside forces will react in ways that help the revolutionary cause. And sometimes, too, those third parties are completely bewildered by these attacks.

This has been the case time after time in the response of the West to terrorist attacks by Islamist revolutionaries. It is hard enough for Westerners to recognize that their attackers actually have a coherent strategy and are not simply mad fanatics motivated by hatred. To accept that these terrorist attacks are not really about Western countries at all, but merely an attempt to use the overreaction of Western countries as a stepping-stone to the seizure of power in the terrorists' own countries, is just too demeaning to bear. For a generation of Americans who take pride in belonging to "the greatest power on Earth," being the unwitting tool in somebody else's strategy is inconceivable, so the United States (and other Western countries) generally fall back on simple-minded explanations like "they hate our values" to explain the attacks.

The first generation of Islamist revolutionaries in the

Arab world emerged in the late 1970s in response to the abject failure of the military regimes to keep their promises about delivering economic growth, military might, rising living standards and the defeat of Israel. In this situation it was inevitable that many younger people would turn to thoughts of revolution, but it was not going to be a Marxist revolution: that particular ideology had been thoroughly discredited by the dictators for whom it had been the guiding star. Instead, large numbers of the young revolutionaries turned to Islamism, which proposed an entirely different route to the same goals of prosperity, military security, social justice (and the ultimate defeat of Israel).

Islamist ideology argued that the patterns of development that had worked for the infidel West were completely inappropriate for Muslim societies. Instead, the right course of action was to ensure that everybody strictly observed all the rules laid down by God (in the rather extremist interpretation of Islam favoured by the Islamists) for the behaviour of good Muslims. And once everybody in the society had stopped smoking, stopped drinking alcohol, stopped listening to music, stopped the disgusting mixing of the sexes in social and work situations; once the men had stopped trimming their beards, and once everybody was living as true Muslims had done in the time of the Prophet, 1,300 years ago—then God would ensure that people in the Muslim countries had the power, prosperity and respect they longed for.

It was magical thinking, of course, but a significant minority of Arab Muslims were desperate enough to be seduced by it. To make revolution a reality, however, they needed bigger numbers. So the first task of any Islamist was to start in his own country and build a popular base of support that would one day be able to put tens or hundreds of thousands of people on the streets, risking their lives to bring the old regime down.

The strategy, as in most revolutionary situations, was terrorism. Partly, terrorism is simply "propaganda of the deed": a way to make yourself and your ideas known to the population when the public media are under government control. But terrorism also creates significant possibilities for pushing the regime into a policy of extreme repression that alienates the public and drives new recruits into the ranks of the Islamists.

Terrorism in the modern style is not an Islamist invention. It is a technique that has been around for at least a century, and revolutionaries of every imaginable variety—the Irish Republican Army, the Tamil Tigers in Sri Lanka, the Symbionese Liberation Army in the United States, the Shining Path in Peru, the Japanese Red Army and the Baader-Meinhof Gang in Germany—have availed themselves of terrorist strategies. Generally they have failed, since terrorism's tactics are far from foolproof. But when you are hopelessly outmatched by the military, political and financial resources of the governments you seek to overthrow, you employ the strategy that's available to you.

Viewed in that context, the Islamist revolutionary movements have made quite effective use of the technique.

Not all Islamist revolutionary movements turned immediately to violence. At the end of the 1980s, for example, many of the Algerian Islamists persuaded themselves that they might actually win power through the ballot box (although they did not believe that democracy was compatible with Islam, and were unforthcoming on their longer-term plans for the Algerian state—a policy caricatured by their critics as "one man, one vote, one time"). Similarly, the main Egyptian Islamist organization, the Muslim Brotherhood, avoided violence during this period and was rewarded by being allowed some marginal participation in the Egyptian political system (through the election to parliament of "independent" candidates who were not permitted to publicly proclaim their membership in the Brotherhood). Extreme violence in Egypt was the domain of two much smaller Islamist groups, Islamic Jihad, which organized the assassination of Egypt's president Anwar Assad in 1981, and the Islamic Group, which waged an insurgency against the Egyptian government in 1992–98 that killed almost eight hundred people. The primary targets of the latter group were Egyptian military and political figures, but towards the end of its campaign it also branched out into killing foreign tourists: seventeen Greek tourists outside their Cairo hotel in 1997, and fifty-eight Western and Japanese tourists in Hatshepsut's temple in Luxor later the same year.

The strategic rationale behind these attacks was much the same as in terrorist campaigns anywhere else in the world. First, they drew the attention of the public to the existence and ideas of the revolutionary organization, in a media environment where it was otherwise very difficult to get the message out. Second, in countries that depended heavily on tourism—more than 5 percent of Egyptian GDP in the late 1990s—attacks on foreign tourists could create great economic hardship by damaging the tourism industry. In terrorism theory, at least, those who lose their jobs because tourists are afraid to come will blame the government for their misfortune rather than the terrorists, and so will be readier to withdraw their consent from the regime and support the revolutionaries.

Two other major Islamist uprisings in the Arab world during this early period were the seizure of the Grand Mosque in Mecca in 1979 and the revolt in Hama in Syria in 1983. In Saudi Arabia it took the army two weeks to take back control of the most sacred site in the Islamic world, and at least five hundred people were killed in the fighting. The revolt in Hama against Syria's secular Ba'athist regime was led by the local Muslim Brotherhood, which had taken a more violent path than its parent organization in Egypt. The fighting in Hama lasted three weeks, much of the city was destroyed, and an estimated 30–40,000 people were killed by the regime's troops. But none of these attempts to spark a revolution, in Egypt, Syria or Saudi Arabia, led to the overthrow of the existing regime and the creation of a government run by Islamists. And in case the message was not clear enough already, the fate of the Islamist uprising in Algeria in the 1990s drove it home.

Except for those who are with us, all others are apostates and deserving of death.

– Attributed to Antar Zouabri, "emir"
of the Islamic Armed Group, 1996–2002[4]

The increasing radicalization and eventual collapse of Islamist opposition to the rule of the army in Algeria during the civil war of 1992–2002 epitomizes the problem faced by Arab revolutionaries in the post-colonial era. In the Algerian independence war of 1954–62 it was obvious who the enemy was: the imperial power, France, and the million French-speaking European settlers in Algeria. For most Algerians the choice was easy, and in the end the French army did not even have to be destroyed in battle. Just make the cost to the French of staying in Algeria too high in lives and in money, and they will eventually cut their losses and go home *because they actually have another home to go to.* Revolutionary victories in several dozen European colonies in the 1950s and 1960s created the myth that revolutionary war, whether fought as a guerrilla war in rural areas or a terrorist war in the cities, was unstoppable, but it really only worked well in the anti-colonial context.

Subsequent decades showed that when later generations of "Third World" revolutionaries tried to use the same techniques against local regimes that had failed to produce either prosperity or democracy in the newly independent countries of Africa, Asia and the Middle East, they generally failed. The enemy in power now consisted of fellow-countrymen, military or civilian, who had wide networks of allies and supporters in the population, making it much harder to organize a mass mobilization against them. Moreover, most of the regime's supporters would stay and fight rather than cut and run, because—except for the very rich with foreign bank accounts—they had no other home to go to. So the success rate in these post-colonial revolutionary wars was very low.

Algeria, which had been ruled by the army since shortly after independence from France, had mass anti-regime protests in 1988 that resulted in a number of political reforms, including the legalization of opposition parties. The army assumed that the public would be so grateful for these reforms that they would vote for its own party, the National Liberation Front. But in the first vote under the new dispensation in 1990, a new Islamist party, the Islamic Salvation Front (FIS), won control of about half of the municipal and provincial assemblies in local elections. It also won a large majority of seats in the first round of voting for a new national parliament in 1991—but that development panicked the military into cancelling the second round of the elections and aborting the democratic process. The army also arrested the main FIS leaders and banned the party.

Algerian Islamists responded with an armed struggle that lasted more than a decade. The FIS rapidly spun off two other Islamist groups that competed with each other in their religious radicalism: the Islamic Salvation Army (which operated mainly in rural areas making guerrilla attacks against government forces) and the Islamic Armed Group (which was primarily city-based and specialized in urban terrorism). Neither of them succeeded, although it took the regime ten years and up to 150,000 deaths to quell the revolt. As the struggle proceeded, relatively mature revolutionary leaders were killed or jailed, and replaced by younger leaders who were more extreme in their ideology and less discriminate in their killing. By 1997 entire villages were being massacred for collaborating with the regime—"Except for those who are with us, all others are apostates and deserving of death"—and the bulk of the population came to the conclusion that the regime, however cruel and corrupt, was more acceptable than the revolutionaries.

By 2005 the war had effectively come to an end in Algeria, and the regime had won. Even before that, various Islamist leaders had concluded that their whole strategy for stimulating revolutions in the Arab world was missing some vital element. Two decades of terrorist attacks in the Middle East, which killed many thousands of people, the vast majority of them Muslim Arabs, had still not created a critical mass of popular support for the Islamist revolutionaries in any Arab country. It is not clear whether the Islamists consciously contrasted this failure of terrorism against domestically based regimes with the earlier successes in comparable struggles against foreign imperialists, but some of them did get to the obvious conclusion. It was high time for a better strategy: what they needed was a foreign —preferably infidel—enemy.

———————●———————

The nations of the infidels have all united against the Muslims. . . . This is a new battle, a great battle, similar to the great battles of Islam like the conquest of Jerusalem. . . . The Crusaders [i.e., the Americans] come out to fight Islam in the name of fighting terrorism.

Osama bin Laden, October 2002[5]

By the late 1990s, Osama bin Laden was a man on the run. Born in Saudi Arabia in 1957 into a family that had become immensely wealthy in the construction business, he became more radical in his religious thinking and more openly critical of existing Arab regimes (including the Saudi royal family) during his time at King Abdulaziz University in 1977–79. He left Saudi Arabia in 1980 to support the mujahedeen who were fighting the Soviet occupation of Afghanistan. First as a volunteer in Pakistan coordinating the flow of money, supplies and arms to the fighters in Afghanistan, later as a leader of foreign fighters inside the country, he spent most of a decade waging jihad against the Russian infidels before Moscow gave up and pulled all its troops out in 1989. Like most of the foreign volunteers, his views were transformed by the experience of fighting alongside Muslims from many other countries in a common struggle against infidel invaders, and it was in 1988 or 1989, in the mujahedeen camps in Afghanistan, that bin Laden created the organization known as al Qaeda ("The Base" or "The Foundation").

What he had learned, like many of his generation, was that the experience of fighting foreign invaders had a powerful unifying and radicalizing effect on people from all over the Muslim world. He also learned that if Islamists win a war against infidel foreign invaders in any Muslim country, they almost automatically win the struggle for domestic power as well. (The Taliban, the Afghan Islamist group closest to bin Laden's own theological views, did not finally defeat their rivals and take power in Kabul until 1996, but it was clear much earlier in the civil war that followed the Russian withdrawal from Afghanistan that the victors would be Islamists of one stripe or another.) So it was very much under the influence of his Afghan experiences that bin Laden formulated the revolutionary strategy that made him famous.

He began to talk in terms of the "near enemy" (the corrupt regimes to be overthrown by Islamist revolutions in Arab and other Muslim countries) and the "far enemy" (the powerful infidel governments that dominated the Muslim world from afar). There was no possibility of overthrowing the "far enemy," but also no need. All you had to do was get the far enemy to invade Muslim countries, as the Russians had invaded Afghanistan, and the results would be the same: radicalization in Muslim countries, a rapid growth in the number of young men wanting to wage jihad, ultimate defeat for the infidel invader, and the establishment of Islamist governments in the countries from which the invaders were finally expelled. Bin Laden was trying to recreate the circumstances that had just brought the Islamists such a striking victory in Afghanistan, after such a long string of revolutionary failures elsewhere. In the end, he was quite successful.

A co-founder of al Qaeda, Egyptian ex-colonel Saif al Adel, later summarized the organization's long-term plans in five consecutive phases under the title "Al Qaeda's Strategy to the Year 2020":

1. Provoke the United States and the West into invading a Muslim country by staging a massive attack or string of attacks on U.S. soil that results in massive civilian casualties.

2. Incite local resistance to occupying forces.

3. Expand the conflict to neighbouring countries, and engage the United States and its allies in a long war of attrition.

4. Convert al Qaeda into an ideology and set of operating principles that can be loosely franchised in other countries without requiring direct

command and control, and via these franchises
incite attacks against the United States and countries allied with the United States until they withdraw from the conflict.

5. The U.S. economy will finally collapse by the year
2020, under the strain of multiple engagements in
numerous places, making the worldwide economic
system, which is dependent on the United States,
also collapse, leading to global political instability,
which will in turn make possible a global jihad led
by al Qaeda. Following the collapse of the United
States and the rest of the Western countries, a
Wahhabi caliphate [one that follows the austere
Saudi Arabian variant of Sunni Islam] will then be
installed across the world.[6]

This document was clearly written in the late 1990s at
the earliest, but is still heavily influenced by the fact and
manner of the mujahedeen's victory over the Soviet Union.
The first three stages of the strategy are an obvious attempt
to relive that triumph by entangling the United States in a
similarly forlorn war, the only difference being that, as
the United States will not obligingly stage an unprovoked
invasion of a Muslim country, it will be necessary to lure it
into this trap by making a mass-casualty attack on the
American homeland.

The fourth phase is a genuinely original plan for a decentralized jihadi organization that is invulnerable precisely

because of its lack of a centre. The franchise model has been al Qaeda's greatest strength—although on some occasions, most notably in the case of the Islamic State in Iraq and al-Sham (ISIS), a franchise has gone down what bin Laden and his companions would have considered the wrong road and has had to be disowned.

The fifth and final stage, of course, is a wish-fulfillment fantasy that reveals the real naïveté behind bin Laden's apparent strategic sophistication. He is more realistic about the strength of the "far enemy" than most of his colleagues, but in the end he too believes in the caricatures of morally superior Muslims who will triumph just because they are in the right, and corrupt and decadent non-Muslims who will be defeated simply because they are evil. The lost Golden Age will return, and then everyone (or the survivors, at least) will live happily ever after.

And there is one key calculation that goes unmentioned not only here but in every document produced by every revolutionary organization that employs terrorist tactics: that bringing death and devastation down on the heads of those whose support the organization wants is the only way it can actually get that support. Most ordinary people would really just like to get on quietly with their lives, but the terrorists deliberately provoke the local regime (or, in al Qaeda's case, a foreign country) in order to make their lives hell. It's a kind of political jiu-jitsu: the revolutionaries make spectacular attacks that don't really do any strategic harm to their opponent, but infuriate the target regime or country to the point that it unleashes massive violence in retaliation—violence that, in the nature of such things, will by and large hurt innocent people the most. Repeat as necessary, until a large enough section of the population has turned to your organization (now posing as the defender of the people) to create the critical mass needed for a revolution.

Just as it is not clear exactly when Saif al-Adel wrote the above document, it is not known exactly when Osama bin Laden finally arrived at the strategy it outlines. Bin Laden returned to Saudi Arabia in 1989, but when Saddam Hussein's Iraq invaded Kuwait in 1990 and threatened the Saudi kingdom, King Fahd allowed American and other Western "infidel" forces to deploy troops on Saudi territory. Outraged, bin Laden denounced the king's decision, and was eventually forced into exile as a result. The only Arab country willing to take him was Sudan, where a military officer called Omar al-Bashir had recently seized power in a coup and imposed Shari'ah law on the country. Bin Laden enjoyed sanctuary in Sudan until 1996, when the United States succeeded in getting him expelled in return for an easing of sanctions on Sudan. He found a new home in Afghanistan, where the Taliban, like-minded Afghan Islamists, had captured Kabul and brought a measure of peace to the south and centre of the country in 1996. They invited bin Laden and his merry men to set up shop there.

It was from Afghanistan that he issued his declaration of war against the West in February 1998, signed by himself, his deputy Ayman al Zawahiri, and three other Islamist leaders and faxed to the newspaper *Al-Quds Al-Arabi* in London. It purportedly came from the World Islamic Front for Combat Against the Jews and Crusaders, and took the form of a fatwa—although none of the signatories possessed the qualifications required to issue such a religious decree binding on all Muslims:

> The ruling to kill the Americans and their allies— civilians and military—is an individual duty for every Muslim who can do it in any country in which it is possible to do it, in order to liberate the al-Aqsa Mosque [in Jerusalem] and the holy mosque [in Mecca] from their grip, and in order for their armies to move out of all the lands of Islam, defeated and unable to threaten any Muslim. This is in accordance with the words of Almighty Allah, "and fight the pagans all together as they fight you all together," and "fight them until there is no more tumult or oppression, and there prevail justice and faith in Allah."[7]

This bizarre concern among men about to commit mass murder with obtaining a religious authorization for their intended actions, even if they had to manufacture it themselves, is actually quite understandable in view of Islam's strong emphasis on the legality (under Shari'ah law) of one's actions. They genuinely felt that they had to produce a legal justification for mass-casualty attacks on American civilians and others before they launched the first of those atrocities, the truck-bomb attacks on the American embassies in Kenya and Tanzania, in August of 1998.

The attacks certainly did produce mass casualties (more than two hundred killed and an estimated four thousand wounded), but only twelve of the fatal casualties were Americans, and the Clinton administration's response was correspondingly modest: merely some cruise missile attacks on Sudan and Afghanistan. To elicit the huge American response that al Qaeda wanted would require a much bigger death toll, and probably a shift of venue to the United States homeland as well, but was that a conclusion that bin Laden reached only after the East African attacks? It's quite likely, as he would have been feeling his way forward in relatively unknown territory. The two years that separate those East African attacks from the vastly more ambitious operation in September 2001 are just about right, in terms of the time he would have needed to draw his conclusions and plan the 9/11 attacks.

One other intriguing question arises about this period, in view of the fact that bin Laden spent the whole time in the camp in southern Afghanistan that his old friend Mullah Mohammed Omar Mansoor ("Mullah Omar"), then the leader of the Taliban, had made available to him. Did he keep Omar informed of his plans? He could have kept him in the dark if he had wished, as the actual preparations for the attacks were all done by bin Laden's al Qaeda colleagues in Europe and the United States, and he controlled his own communications. We will probably never know the answer for certain, but a consideration of the two men's relative positions suggests that bin Laden would have been unwise to tell Omar what he was planning to do.

From bin Laden's point of view, the 9/11 attacks made good sense. He was a homeless revolutionary with big ideas but little in the way of accomplishments, and the revolution he sought might never get off the ground if he could not somehow provoke the United States into invading a Muslim country. The country in question would certainly be Afghanistan, since the U.S. would quickly work out who had ordered the attack and Afghanistan was his base. Bin Laden had nothing to lose, and a great deal to gain, if the United States invaded Afghanistan.

Now consider the position of Mullah Omar in 2001. He no longer sought a revolution; he was already in power, and he was engaged in putting the full Islamist programme into effect in Afghanistan. An American invasion might be advantageous for bin Laden's comparable project, but it would drive the Taliban from power, destroy all their achievements, and send them back to the hills as mere guerrillas for another decade or more, even if they won in the end. The two men may have been as close as brothers, but in the circumstances it would have required a great leap of faith for bin Laden to have confided his specific plans to Omar beforehand. He probably didn't do so.

So the attacks went ahead as planned on September 11, 2001, and some three thousand people, the great majority

of them Americans, died on live television before the hor-
rified eyes of their fellow citizens. It all seems inevitable in
retrospect, and in this case it probably was, once bin Laden
got his Big Idea. A great deal of what followed did not con-
form to his expectations, but in the broadest sense he got
what he bargained for.

CHAPTER 3

———•———

JIHAD: THE AFGHAN PHASE, 2001–2003

There was a popular conversation game in the United States in the aftermath of the 9/11 attacks called "What would Al Gore have done?" Would things have turned out better had the Florida vote recounts gone in Gore's favour in the 2000 election, so that Gore would have been in the White House in September 2001? They would probably have gone better in the long run, but nobody could have handled the immediate American response to the attack better than George W. Bush and his senior colleagues.

We will probably never know the name of the evil genius who came up with the idea of attacking the Twin Towers in New York City with aircraft, but it certainly met bin Laden's requirement for a terrorist extravaganza so spectacular that the American government would be compelled to respond in the way that al Qaeda wanted. After the damp squib of President Clinton's response to the bombings of the American embassies in East Africa in 1998, it was clear to the plotters that the majority of the victims in this case had to be Americans, and that there had to be a lot of them. But it was not enough that many Americans be killed in a terrorist attack; they had to be killed in a dramatic and visually unforgettable way, and on home soil.

This is actually quite hard to arrange. You can bomb some huge political rally or sporting event and cause mass casualties, but you will probably not get the toll up into the thousands, and the nature of the pictures—shots of people fleeing, shots of people down, perhaps a shaky video clip of the flash of the explosion—will not adequately convey the scale of the event anyway. Attacks on mass transport offer crowds of potential victims and the possibility of dramatic collisions, crashes or sinkings, but you can't count on anybody getting good footage of it at the right moment (unless you shoot your own), and the pictures shot later by the networks will be identical to the sort of stuff they churn out after any other train or plane crash. How are you going to trademark this as a *terrorist* attack, so huge and uniquely horrible that something very big must be done about it?

Numbers of dead alone may not do it. The 9/11 attacks killed about three thousand people, but another three thousand Americans died in road accidents in the same month (and another three thousand died of gunshot wounds). What counted most were the images, and the al Qaeda planner chose well: civilian airliners sailing serenely across a clear blue sky and smashing into arrogantly tall buildings; those same buildings in flames in the very heartland of global finance; hundred-storey towers collapsing on their trapped occupants in a way that nobody had ever seen before. It created exactly the sense of utter shock that al Qaeda needed, and made it inevitable that the U.S. government would have to invade Afghanistan in order to root out the authors of the atrocity. But it did not actually mandate how Washington had to do the job.

The people around President Bush happened to know the Middle East well. Vice-President Dick Cheney, Secretary of State Colin Powell and Defense Secretary Donald Rumsfeld had all served in senior posts under his father, President George H.W. Bush, during the first Gulf War a decade before: they had met all the Arab leaders many times, they knew the terrain, and they even knew a fair amount about Arab politics. It's unlikely that they knew a lot about the theory and practice of terrorism (except Powell, who would undoubtedly have been taught it as a young officer), but they were all people whose experience would lead them to ask the right question: What did al Qaeda's planners want America to do next? And the answer was obvious: invade Afghanistan.

They would certainly have known from history that invading Afghanistan is generally a bad idea. It's quite easy to conquer the provinces and take control of Kabul; pretty well every invading army has got that far. But it's very hard for a foreign army to stay in Afghanistan with any comfort for more than a year or two, because the Afghans hate being invaded (it has happened too often in their history), and almost every male Afghan, at least in rural areas, has access to firearms. On the other hand, American public opinion would accept nothing less than an invasion. The American media, of course, were demanding decisive military action by lunchtime tomorrow at the very latest, but the White House held its fire and made its plans.

The most important element in the plan came from George Tenet, a Democratic appointee whom Bush had the sense to leave in place as director of the Central Intelligence Agency. Only two days after the New York and Washington attacks, Tenet proposed that there should be no conventional invasion of Afghanistan at all. Instead, CIA paramilitary teams would enter the country secretly and buy up allies among the various tribal forces in the north of the country that were still resisting the authority of Mullah Omar's Taliban regime in Kabul. They would bring in communications equipment to keep those tribal forces in constant contact with their new American allies, and later they would be joined by U.S. Special Forces teams whose main task was target designation for American aircraft. Then, when everything was ready, U.S. Air Force and Navy planes would bomb the bejesus out of the Taliban forces in the trenches facing the various ethnic groups that made up the Northern Alliance (Tajiks, Uzbeks, Turkmen and Hazaras), the northern militias would advance, and the fighting should be practically over before American ground forces arrived in the country.

It worked exactly according to plan. The so-called

Northern Alliance was barely a real alliance at all: out-numbered two-to-one by Taliban troops, the various ethnic militias often fought each other, and the one widely respected leader of the alliance, Ahmed Shah Massoud, had been killed by an al Qaeda suicide team posing as television journalists two days before 9/11. But the first ten-man CIA team arrived in northern Afghanistan on September 26 bearing $3 million in cash and promising American air support to General Mohammed Fahim, Massoud's successor. American aircraft began bombing al Qaeda and Taliban targets in Afghanistan on October 7, although they did not spend much time on the Taliban troops facing the Northern Alliance until the other CIA teams and U.S. Special Forces troops were in position all along the 550-mile (800-kilometre) front line that stretched across northern Afghanistan.

That took a further month, and the Bush administration, despite its unilateralist instincts, spent the time gaining a form of legal authority for the attack from the U.N. Security Council and building a coalition of allies for the job of peacekeeping in a post-Taliban Afghanistan. Even the bombing was done with extra care, avoiding civilian casualties as much as possible. One estimate is that the United States dropped eighteen thousand bombs on Afghanistan during the five weeks of the war but killed only five thousand civilians. Any ratio lower than one bomb to one dead civilian is evidence of a policy of strict restraint in the choice of targets.

Finally, in early November, six CIA political teams and a larger number of Special Forces target designation teams were in place on the front line, and massive U.S. air power was unleashed on the Taliban troops facing the Northern Alliance. The bombing was so accurate and so relentless that the Taliban troops broke and abandoned their positions in many places along the front. Some Taliban commanders had already been bribed to switch sides when the offensive began, and when they kept their promises the Taliban retreat swiftly turned into a rout. Mazar-i-Sharif, the largest city in the north, fell on November 9, and Kabul itself was evacuated by the Taliban regime on November 12. When the Northern Alliance's troops entered the capital on the following day, there were still only 110 CIA officers and 316 U.S. Special Forces personnel in the whole country.

By December 7, with the fall of Mullah Omar's headquarters in the southwestern city of Kandahar, the Taliban regime was history. There were a few disappointments: Omar got away on his motorcycle, and there were strong suspicions that Osama bin Laden and many of his senior colleagues survived the huge air strikes during the December battle of Tora Bora, a cave complex in the mountains along the Pakistani border, and escaped into Pakistan. But as a whole the operation was a remarkable success.

———————•———————

If American policy in Afghanistan had continued in the same prudent and pragmatic mode, the next step would have been the construction of a new Afghan regime, preferably with a democratic veneer, that actually depended on the self-serving support of the various northern warlords and of comparable Pashtun leaders, ex-Taliban or not, from the south of the country. (The Pashtuns, amounting to about 40 percent of the population, had been the main and almost the only source of support for the Taliban.) Then, as soon as possible and certainly within a couple of years, Western troops would have gone home, leaving only a large and steady flow of money for the new masters of the country as an inducement for them to remain cooperative.

It would not have been an elegant solution, but that is precisely how Afghanistan had been ruled for most of its history, and it would have been at least as stable as any alternative solution. It would also have deprived Islamists of the opportunity to claim that the West was at war with Islam.

The "war on terror" would have continued in some form, for the American public would have insisted on that. With the Afghan victory under his belt, however, Bush could have explained to Americans that Afghanistan had been the one target in this war against which it made sense to use conventional military force. There had actually been physical al Qaeda bases there under the protection of a sovereign state, so a real war was necessary to destroy them (although mercifully few American soldiers had been involved in the actual fighting). But terrorists are in general civilians living among other civilians, and the appropriate tools for dealing with this sort of threat are police forces, intelligence services, and of course better security measures at home.

"Go home, folks, the show's over," President Bush should have said in his State of the Union message in January 2002. "The war on terror is now moving into a second, much longer phase that will be largely invisible. We'll be working hard to track down and eliminate the remaining al Qaeda members, but it will be a mostly secret war and even when we have a big success you may not always hear about it." If he had said that, the history of the early twenty-first century would have been considerably altered. But he said something quite different, and utterly unexpected. He said he was going to invade Iraq.

I expected to go back to a round of meetings [on September 12, 2001] examining what the next attacks could be, what our vulnerabilities were, what we could do about them in the short term. Instead, I walked into a series of discussions about Iraq. At first I was incredulous that we were talking about something other than getting al Qaeda. Then I realized . . . that [Secretary of Defense Donald] Rumsfeld and [Deputy Secretary of Defense Paul] Wolfowitz were going to try to take advantage of this tragedy to promote their agenda about Iraq. Since the beginning of the administration, they had been pressing for a war in Iraq.

Former White House counter-terrorism chief Richard A. Clarke[8]

What Bush actually said in his address was that states like Iraq, Iran and North Korea and their terrorist allies constituted an "axis of evil," arming to threaten the peace of the world. These three countries had virtually nothing in common except that they had all successfully defied American power at some point in the past. Iraq was a secular Arab dictatorship; Iran was a theocratic revolutionary state that had recently fought a bloody eight-year war with Iraq; and North Korea was a hereditary Communist hermit kingdom at the far end of Asia. Bush did not explicitly say that he was going to invade them all, but he was certainly suggesting that something would have to be done about them. And it was quite clear that the first candidate for the treatment would be Iraq.

A very charitable interpretation of Bush's choices would be that all three of these countries had been working on nuclear weapons at some point, and that the president feared they might "provide these arms to terrorists" to attack the United States. (North Korea was indeed trying to develop nuclear weapons, and would actually test one in 2006; Iran was clandestinely working on them too, probably in response to the Pakistani nuclear tests of 1998, although it is not clear that this was known to the American intelligence services until later in 2002; and Saddam Hussein in Iraq had been trying to build nuclear weapons during the 1980–88 Iran-Iraq war—but his nuclear facilities had been comprehensively dismantled by the United Nations Special Commission and International Atomic

Energy Agency inspectors after his defeat in the first Gulf War of 1990–91.)

But there was no discussion of possible Iraqi "weapons of mass destruction" in those early cabinet conversations in Washington about an invasion of Iraq. The real reason that it rose to the top of the target list was the great influence of the neo-conservatives in the Bush administration. The "neo-cons" believed that a unique opportunity to dominate the planet in the service of American capital and American democratic ideals had been given to the United States when the former Soviet Union collapsed in 1991. However, it had been frittered away by the reluctance of the Clinton administrations (1992–2000) to exploit U.S. military strength to the full. They therefore argued that one or more demonstrations of American resolve were needed, in the form of short, successful wars against hostile regimes, in order to restore global respect for American power. Afghanistan had been a success, but it was too quick and easy, against an opponent with little conventional military power, to serve the neo-conservatives' purposes. Iraq, which did have large armed forces but not very effective ones, would be an ideal venue for the necessary demonstration. Going along with this idea was Bush's biggest blunder—but it represented salvation for Osama bin Laden.

Bin Laden's masterstroke had not worked out as planned at all. The United States had responded to his attack by invading Afghanistan, as he anticipated, but it did it in such a way that his expectation of a long, bloody guerrilla war with lots of Muslim casualties, like the one the Soviet Union had to fight during its ten-year occupation of Afghanistan, was not fulfilled. American troops did end up staying for ten years and more, but even so their total military casualties in Afghanistan were only 2,312 dead. Soviet fatal casualties in a comparable period in 1979–89 were 14,453, more than six times as high. The difference between the Soviet and American occupations in non-military casualties is even greater, with civilian deaths twenty or more times higher under the Russians. The much lower American figures were a direct consequence of the relatively circumspect way in which U.S. military power was employed in Afghanistan both during and after the invasion. Bin Laden did not get the holocaust of innocent Muslim victims he had been expecting. In short, 9/11 failed in its primary purpose.

We have no reliable information about bin Laden's activities and whereabouts in the months immediately after his escape from Afghanistan. He was presumably in Pakistan, in deep cover and not daring to use any electronic means of communication, but we do not know whether Pakistan's Inter-Services Intelligence agency (ISI) was protecting him at this stage; nor do we know when he was moved to his long-term hiding place in Abbottabad. He would not have been in direct contact with what remained of his network of collaborators within and beyond the Arab world, and most of his information about what was happening in the world would have come from Pakistan's English-language press. It would not have been positive news for him—but Bush's State of the Union speech in January 2002 would have cheered him up immensely. He was going to be given a free second kick at the can.

———————•———————

All of us are saying: "Hey, United States, we don't think this is a very good idea."

King Abdullah II of Jordan, July 2002[9]

Only in the traumatized United States was there wide-spread popular acceptance of the rationale President Bush offered for going to war: "to disarm Iraq of weapons of mass destruction, to end Saddam Hussein's support for terrorism, and to free the Iraqi people." (In fact there were no Iraqi weapons of mass destruction, Saddam Hussein had no links whatever to al Qaeda or any other Islamist group, and the Iraqi people turned out to be deeply divided about being "freed" by the Americans.) U.S. allies in the Arab world were unanimous in arguing, publicly or privately, that this was in fact an extremely stupid and dangerous idea. Even in Britain, where Prime Minister Tony Blair was so dedicated to the Anglo-American "special relationship" that he had his first ambassador, Sir Christopher Meyer, instructed "to get up the arse of the White House and stay there,"[10] there was much public criticism about the way the intelligence was being "cooked" to provide justifications for the invasion. Other long-standing American allies like France and Germany flatly refused to take any part in the operation, which they rightly judged to be contrary to international law. And despite a major diplomatic effort Blair and Bush failed to persuade the U.N. Security Council to authorize the invasion of Iraq. So, by starting the war anyway, both men technically made themselves liable to prosecution as war criminals—not that there was any real risk of that happening.

The hubris of the neo-cons in the Bush administration, who were the main moving force behind the enterprise, was astounding. They believed that Islamist terrorism in the Arab world could best be defeated by forcibly injecting democracy into Iraq and watching the infection spread. Moreover, they believed the new Arab democracies would automatically be pro-American. As Paul Wolfowitz assured Congress just before the invasion:

> These are Arabs, 23 million of the most educated people in the Arab world, who are going to welcome us as lib-erators. And when the message gets out to the whole Arab world, it's going to be a powerful counter to Osama bin Laden . . . It will be a great step forward.[11]

Fantasy images of grateful Arabs strewing flowers at the feet of the American invaders were a recurrent feature in the self-deceiving discourse of the neo-cons. The country's 23 million people were indeed among the best-educated in the Arab world—oil wealth had enabled the ruling Ba'ath Party to build a welfare state that made good education and decent health care available free to its citizens, and even accorded women equal footing in the law and the workplace—but Iraqis were far from a unified people. Twenty percent of them were not even Arabs: the Kurds of the north spoke a different language entirely and nurtured a desire for independence that made them see Americans as potential allies. Much trickier was the fact that about 20 percent of the population were Sunni Arabs, while an absolute majority, 60 percent, were Shia Muslims. Yet the Sunni Arab minority ran everything and had done so for hundreds of years.

Saddam Hussein was a Sunni (though not a particularly devout one for most of his life), and so had been every other governor, king and president since the Ottoman Empire took the territory from Persia in 1533. The great majority of the Arabic-speaking population remained Shia, but Sunnis so dominated the public sphere in Iraq under Turkish and British rule and in the forty-five years of independence before the American invasion that many Sunnis did not even realize they were a minority in Iraq. (Statistics on the sectarian loyalties of the population were not publicly available under Saddam's rule, for obvious reasons.) So the first thing the U.S. occupation administration would face once it controlled the country was the bitter resistance of the Sunnis whose centuries-long rule it had overthrown, and the relentless drive of the Shia majority to exploit the opportunity created by the invasion to install a new Shia political supremacy in the country. "Democracy," in the American sense of the word, was not a high priority for either side.

Iraq was actually far better terrain for bin Laden's strategy than Afghanistan, which was an extremely poor, non-Arab country on the far periphery of the Middle East. Iraq, by contrast, was mostly Arab in population, a major oil exporter, and located in the heart of the Arab world. The head of al Qaeda just hadn't been in a position earlier to trick the United States into invading Iraq or some other major country in the Arab heartland, so he had made do with what was available. He must have been astounded at his luck when President Bush declared his intention to take down Saddam Hussein.

Bin Laden was not able to influence events in Iraq in any way, but that was not necessary. The highly decentralized "franchise" model he had created in al Qaeda guaranteed that men with the right beliefs, skills and goals would appear in Iraq to exploit the immense opportunity that an American invasion would create. And at this point, bin Laden essentially faded back into an advisory and symbolic role, although he lived on in hiding, far from the action, for another eight years.

The invasion of Iraq by 148,000 American and 45,000 British troops (accompanied by 2,000 Australians and a few Poles) began on March 19, 2003. The conquest of Iraq was just as easy as the American planners expected it to be. By the time a flight-suited President Bush flew out to the aircraft carrier *Abraham Lincoln* to declare an end to major combat operations (with a banner saying "Mission Accomplished" prominently displayed in the background for the television cameras), only 138 American soldiers had been killed. The "kill-ratio," as is often the case when one side tries to fight without air cover, had been around a hundred-to-one in favour of the U.S. Army. American military planners were assuming that they would be able to draw down the occupation force in Iraq to only thirty thousand soldiers by the end of the year—but there had been a striking lack of Iraqis throwing flowers.

CHAPTER 4

•

JIHAD: THE IRAQI PHASE, 2003–2006

The invasion of Iraq in 2003 came at a time when the Islamist movement in the Arab world was at an ebb. It had been entirely suppressed in Syria, and was in the final stages of losing the long civil war in Algeria. In Egypt the Muslim Brotherhood was collaborating with the dictatorship of Hosni Mubarak in exchange for being allowed a shadowy existence in politics (seventeen "independent" candidates were elected to parliament in the 2000 election) and a somewhat more visible role in providing social services in the poorest parts of the cities, but the more radical groups that had engaged in terrorist attacks in the 1980s and 1990s had been stamped out. And in Iraq there was no Islamist movement to speak of: they were all either dead or in exile.

Al Qaeda had no members and few contacts in the country, and other Islamist organizations like the Muslim Brotherhood were also largely absent. Saddam Hussein's police state had ruthlessly hunted down and killed Islamist activists in the Sunni community. And, being an equal opportunity oppressor, Saddam dealt with Shia religious leaders who grew too prominent in the same way. So the earliest resistance to the American occupation came mostly from army officers and soldiers who had just taken their uniforms off and gone home, in the "Sunni triangle" west of Baghdad.

They had gone home because in May 2003 the newly appointed head of the "Coalition Provisional Authority," retired American diplomat L. Paul Bremer III, disbanded the entire Iraqi army and police force. He also banned all senior Ba'ath Party members from future employment in government service, together with anyone in the top three management layers of government ministries, government-run corporations, universities and hospitals who had been a party member at all. (As in the former Communist states of Eastern Europe, membership in the ruling party had been a requirement of promotion to senior rank in these institutions, so he was dismissing the entire top management of all these organizations, although few of them would actually have been Ba'athist activists in any meaningful sense.)

These were Bremer's own decisions, so far as is known, and not imposed on him by the Bush administration. In effect he was not only putting the entire Sunni Arab elite out of work (for most of these jobs under Saddam were reserved for that elite), but also gutting the only two institutions, the army and the police, that at least in theory rose above mere sectarian concerns. He threw half a million people, most of them with weapons training, serious organizational abilities, or both, out on the street in the most humiliating way imaginable—and then was surprised by what they did next.

Even if Bremer had not done what he did, Iraq would likely have produced a serious resistance movement to the American occupation. It was as if a completely different army from a different United States had arrived in Iraq. Instead of the low profile and deliberate restraint of the U.S. forces in Afghanistan, Iraq got an American army that treated the country like a free-fire zone. It was true at the beginning, and remained true for years, that any American soldier could kill any Iraqi for any reason—or none—and get away with it. This reckless behaviour was accompanied by absolutely massive corruption: of the $40 billion that was made available for reconstruction in the year after the invasion (frozen Iraqi funds held in foreign banks, and money voted by the U.S. Congress), less than $10 billion was actually spent on reconstruction. The rest went in cost-plus contracts to American contractors with good White House connections, on deals with Iraqi contractors that involved huge kickbacks, and in straightforward, industrial-scale theft by Americans and Iraqis alike.

Iraq was awash in cash—in dollar bills. Piles and piles of money. We played football with some of the bricks of $100 bills before delivery. It was a wild-west, crazy atmosphere the likes of which none of us had ever experienced.

Frank Willis, former senior official, Coalition Provisional Authority

American law was suspended, Iraqi law was suspended, and Iraq basically became a free fraud zone. In a free fire zone

you can shoot at anybody you want. In a free fraud zone you
can steal anything you like. And that was what they did.

Alan Grayson, Florida-based attorney prosecuting CPA corruption[12]

The consequence of all this corruption was that there was practically no improvement in living conditions in Iraq to compensate for all the inconveniences and humiliations of the foreign occupation. Four years after the arrival of U.S troops, Baghdad was still getting only six hours of electricity a day; even today, Iraqi living standards are far below what they were in Saddam Hussein's heyday. So one can easily imagine the gradual development of a resistance movement against the occupation among disgruntled Iraqis over a period of a few years. In fact, it took only a couple of weeks, and the blame for that remains with L. Paul Bremer III for his demented decision to disband the entire army and police force and purge all former Ba'ath Party members from the bureaucracy. He had unwittingly imposed a social revolution on the country, driving the Sunni Arab minority from power after five centuries on top, and creating a reservoir of half a million Sunni ex-soldiers and ex-bureaucrats with a deep grievance against the occupation authorities and lots of time on their hands.

———————•———————

The very earliest clashes were spontaneous, like the unarmed demonstration in late April 2003 by students in the Sunni city of Fallujah against the takeover of a local high school as a base for American soldiers. Shots were heard off in the distance, the nervous U.S. troops opened fire from the roof of the school, and thirteen students were killed. But by May the first deliberate attacks against American soldiers were taking place, mainly in Sunni areas in and around Baghdad and in the smaller Sunni cities of Fallujah and Tikrit. At first these usually consisted of ambush operations in which small groups of guerrillas would open fire at passing American vehicle convoys, together with the planting of some primitive IEDs (Improvised Explosive Devices) by the roadsides. The American occupation authorities dismissed these resisters as "dead-enders" who would soon fade away, but in fact the attacks grew quickly in scale and complexity: by mid-summer the U.S. army was losing an average of one soldier killed and seven wounded each day.

We are going to fight them and impose our will on them and we will capture them or, if necessary, kill them until we have imposed law and order on this country.

L. Paul Bremer III, June 30, 2003[13]

Bring 'em on!

President George W. Bush, July 2, 2003[14]

I think all foreigners should stop interfering in the internal affairs of Iraq.

Deputy Defense Secretary Paul Wolfowitz, Mosul, Iraq, July 21, 2003[15]

I think we have to recognize that as time goes on, being occupied becomes a problem.

L Paul Bremer III, October 26, 2003[16]

The insurgency took a major step up on August 19, when a massive truck bomb was driven up to the Canal Hotel in Baghdad, the headquarters of the United Nations Assistance Mission in Iraq that had been created only five days earlier, and exploded outside the office occupied by U.N. Special Representative in Iraq Sérgio Vieira de Mello. Twenty-two people were killed in the blast, including Vieira de Mello, and more than a hundred were wounded. As a result, the United Nations withdrew most of its six hundred staff from Iraq. It was not the first truck bombing in Iraq—the Jordanian embassy had been struck on August 7, killing seventeen people—but it was the first suicide bombing. It was also puzzling: why was the Iraqi resistance wasting its time attacking the United Nations?

There was no answer at the time, but in the following year a Jordanian called Abu Musab al Zarqawi, the leader of an Islamist revolutionary group, claimed credit for the attack. Zarqawi's explanation for targeting the United Nations made much of the United Nations' "gift" of Palestine to the Jews "so they can rape the land and humiliate our people," but his specific grievance against Vieira de Mello was one that only an Islamist would harbour. He explained that the U.N. Special Representative deserved to die because in a previous posting he had helped East Timor win its independence back from Muslim-majority Indonesia, which was a crime against the integrity of the Muslim lands that would one day belong to the refounded Islamic caliphate.

Zarqawi was born into poverty and Osama bin Laden into great wealth, but there are striking parallels in their ideas and their life histories. Like bin Laden, Zarqawi went to Afghanistan in the 1980s to wage jihad against the infidel occupiers, but being nine years younger than the founder of al Qaeda he got there only as the Soviet troops were pulling out, and saw no action. He met bin Laden and made a positive impression on him, although even then they had major differences about strategy: he disagreed with bin Laden's focus on the "far enemy," arguing that the priority was to establish an Islamic state on Arab soil. He then returned to Jordan and founded his own militant Islamist group, Jund al Sham.

Zarqawi was imprisoned by the Jordanian government in 1992, after guns and explosives were found in his home, and was only released seven years later in a general amnesty after the death of King Hussein. He immediately set about planning a terrorist attack that would kill hundreds of foreigners celebrating the millennium new year in the Radisson SAS Hotel in Amman, but the plot was discovered and Zarqawi fled to Pakistan and thence to Afghanistan—where he met again with bin Laden and other al Qaeda leaders in late 1999.

There was no going back to Jordan for Zarqawi any more, and bin Laden agreed to give him "seed money" (the figure $200,000 has been mentioned) to set up his own training camp near Herat and the Iranian border for the new group Jama'at al-Tawhid wal-Jihad (Organization for Monotheism and Jihad). It was from this seed that ISIS ultimately grew, but it had barely taken root when it had to be dug up again and moved to another country. Various Jordanian recruits arrived at the Herat camp, but their training was soon interrupted by the American response to al Qaeda's attack on the United States in September 2001. The camp was destroyed by air attacks and Zarqawi escaped, wounded, across the Iranian border, where he reportedly received medical treatment in the Iranian city of Mashhad. His whereabouts in 2002 are subject to much debate, but he was most likely setting up a clandestine camp in Syria from which he planned to send Islamist fighters into Iraq once the much advertised American invasion happened. As indeed he did, once the occupation was in place.

Zarqawi's rapid rise to pre-eminence among the Islamist fighters who went to Iraq owed a great deal to U.S. Secretary of State Colin Powell's depiction of him as al Qaeda's man in Iraq in the period just before the American invasion. American propagandists, trying to create some link between Saddam Hussein and al Qaeda, had seized upon a report by Kurdish intelligence that al Qaeda had funded a base in Iraqi Kurdistan for a new Islamist group called Ansar al Islam. When the latter merged with a group of Jordanian Islamists who were in touch with Zarqawi, the Kurdish secret service leapt to the conclusion that Ansar al Islam's dealings with al Qaeda were conducted via Zarqawi. Powell then used that report and turned Zarqawi into a terrorist megastar in his presentation to the United Nations just weeks before the war.

Iraq today harbors a deadly terrorist network headed by Abu Musab Al-Zarqawi, an associate and collaborator of Osama bin Laden and his Al Qaeda lieutenants. . . . When our coalition ousted the Taliban, the Zarqawi network helped establish another poison and explosive training-center camp. And this camp is located in northeastern Iraq. . . .

Those helping to run this camp are Zarqawi lieutenants operating in northern Kurdish areas outside Saddam Hussein's controlled Iraq [but] Zarqawi's activities are not confined to this small corner of north east Iraq. He travelled to Baghdad in May 2002 for medical treatment, staying in the capital of Iraq for two months while he recuperated to fight another day. During this stay, nearly two dozen extremists converged on Baghdad and established a base of operations there. These al Qaeda affiliates based in Baghdad now coordinate the movement of people, money and supplies into and throughout Iraq for his network, and they have now been operating freely in the capital for more than eight months. . . . We know these affiliates are connected to Zarqawi because they remain even today in regular contact with his direct subordinates. . . . From his terrorist network in Iraq, Zarqawi can direct his network in the Middle East and beyond.

U.S. Secretary of State Colin Powell's speech to
the UN Security Council on Iraq, February 5, 2003[17]

Almost none of this was true. Zarqawi was not then a member of al Qaeda, nor was he in Iraq in 2002. There were no al Qaeda affiliates in Iraq, nor was Zarqawi running a "terrorist network" there. The whole story was concocted to provide a justification for the American invasion. But when Zarqawi showed up in Iraq in 2003, his reputation preceded him, and he quickly emerged as the leader of the foreign jihadis who were flocking into the country to take advantage of the invasion.

The bulk of the resistance activity in Iraq, including almost all the attacks on U.S. troops, continued to be carried out by Sunni Arab Iraqis through the latter half of 2003, and by November an average of three American soldiers were being killed each day. Zarqawi's organization took relatively little part in these activities, preferring to stage specific high-profile attacks on targets that had major political significance. An example was the car bombing outside the Imam Ali Mosque in Najaf, considered by Shia Muslims to be Islam's third-holiest site, just after Friday prayers on August 29. At least eighty-four people were killed in the blast, including Ayatollah Sayed Mohammed Baqir al Hakim and fifteen of his bodyguards. Hakim was one of the most senior Iraqi ayatollahs and had spent the latter part of Saddam's rule in exile in Iran. Indeed, it was Hakim who created the Badr Brigade, made up of Shia exiles from Iraq who volunteered to fight alongside the Iranians during the Iran-Iraq war. Since his return to Iraq in 2003, he had begun to call for the abandonment of anti-American violence, at least for the moment, in order to give the interim governing council appointed by the American occupation authorities a chance to show its worth.

That call for restraint could account for why Hakim became a target of Zarqawi's wrath—but it could also simply have been the fact that he was a prominent Shia leader. Zarqawi was a takfiri, one whose interpretation of the Quran led him to believe that it was legitimate to declare Muslims "apostates" for their deviant beliefs and then kill them. In his view, all Shias fell into the category of apostates, so Iraq was a target-rich environment for him.

Saddam Hussein was captured by U.S. forces in December, and the number of attacks carried out by the resistance dropped significantly in the following months, even though the ex-dictator had not been involved in the enterprise in any way. Then the country exploded in April 2004. There were major uprisings both in the Sunni city of Fallujah and in the Shia holy cities of Karbala and Najaf. Zarqawi was not directly involved in any of these uprisings, but they brought to a head his dispute with Osama bin Laden over the appropriate tactics for jihad. In essence, bin Laden was not keen on killing fellow Muslims and instinctively preferred a "broad front" approach that even extended to Sunni-Shia cooperation against the American occupiers in Iraq. While there were irreconcilable differences between the two groups, those could be left to be sorted out (by killing if necessary) after the infidels had been defeated. Zarqawi, on the other hand, quite apart from his takfiri hatred of Shias, feared that any collaboration between the Sunni and the Shia resistance forces could indeed result in a "broad front"—but one that would smooth over the differences by becoming secular and nationalist, and leaving religion and jihad out of the picture. That was not the war he wanted to fight.

———————— • ————————

The Sunni uprising in Fallujah began on March 31 when a vehicle carrying four American contractors strayed into the city centre and was set upon by a mob. The contractors were killed, and a video was shot of their bodies being burned, their heads being kicked off by the crowd, and two of the charred bodies being strung up, headless, handless and footless, over the stream of traffic crossing the Euphrates bridge, and left there for hours. It was an action well calculated to infuriate the American occupation authorities, and they rose to the bait, declaring that they would seize and occupy Fallujah unless the citizens handed over the people guilty of the atrocity. "What is coming is the destruction of anti-coalition forces in

Fallujah," growled Lieut.-Col. Brennan Byrne, commander of the 1st Battalion, 5th Marine Regiment. "They have two choices: submit or die." Obviously nobody in Fallujah was going to hand over the guilty parties, even in the unlikely event that they were still in the city, so in practice the U.S. Marines and supporting army units were committed to the street-by-street conquest of a hostile Arab city of 300,000 people. The young men of Fallujah would die like flies before the huge firepower and trained infantry brought against them by the United States, but they would fight anyway, and quite a few Americans would die too.

Five days later, just an hour and a half's drive from Fallujah, the Mahdi Army, the Shia militia founded by Muqtada al Sadr, took control of the holy city of Karbala, and other Mahdi forces seized four other Shia-majority cities in the south of Iraq. It was the first time that Shia Arabs had openly confronted the American occupation, but Sadr, son of the martyred Grand Ayatollah Mohammad Sadeq al Sadr, who had been murdered by Saddam Hussein, was determined not to yield until the U.S. agreed to early elections for an Iraqi government. To put it very simplistically, the minority Sunnis were fighting to recover lost privileges, while the Shias were fighting to get a free vote in which their majority status would at last be recognized and rewarded. But it was possible for the two sects to have a loose alliance against the American occupation forces in the meantime.

After five days of heavy fighting in Fallujah, which caused hundreds of civilian casualties, the Marines had taken only a quarter of the city and were ordered to stop. Fighting continued to flare up sporadically until the end of April, when U.S. forces were entirely withdrawn from the city and it fell completely under insurgent control. Many other Sunni towns around Baghdad fell under rebel control at the same time—and the Sunni fighters in Fallujah sent aid to Sadr's besieged Shia forces in Karbala, Najaf and Kufa. As the U.S. forces surrounding the Shia cities ground slowly forward, trying to kill the ill-trained militiamen who were defending the holy cities without damaging them too much, posters of Moqtada al Sadr began to appear in Sunni areas, put up by Sunnis who admired his stand against the Americans. As Zarqawi had feared, a joint Sunni-Shia insurgency that stressed nationalism and not religion was becoming possible in Iraq. It had to be stopped, and the only way was to instigate a Sunni-Shia civil war.

It was necessary to *instigate* such a war, because it would not have just happened of its own accord. Although the provinces that ultimately became Iraq had been ruled by Sunni appointees of the Ottoman Empire for hundreds of years, there was little history of violent conflict between Sunnis and Shias. Indeed, the majority of the Ba'ath Party's founders in Iraq in the early 1950s were Shias. The party's official policies were socialist, secular and pan-Arab, a platform that eventually led to many Shia members leaving it because as Shias they were not interested in the unification of the Arab countries into a single state that would have a large Sunni majority. However, the Shias moved no further than the Iraqi Communist Party (which was also socialist and secular). Under Saddam Hussein, from the 1970s onward, the upper ranks of the Ba'ath Party, and likewise the senior officers of the army, became heavily Sunni, because Saddam operated by building a support network within the Sunni community. But it is a myth (although a comforting one for the Americans who ran the occupation) that Iraq was a sectarian powder keg that was bound to explode once the dictator was removed. It was the divide-and-rule tactics of the occupation authorities and Zarqawi's deliberate provocations that pushed Iraq over the edge.

It was also in the spring of 2004 that Zarqawi's organization began taking Western hostages, dressing them in orange jumpsuits that mimicked those worn by Muslim prisoners in American hands at Guantanamo and elsewhere, beheading them, and making the videos available on the Internet. Details of the abuse of Arab prisoners by American soldiers at Abu Ghraib prison, including allegations of rape and murder, had just been released when Abu Musab al Zarqawi appeared personally in a video with four other men whose faces were hidden by keffiyehs or balaclavas and a hostage in an orange jumpsuit, an American civilian named Nick Berg. Claiming that he was acting in retaliation for the horrors at Abu Ghraib, Zarqawi then proceeded to cut Berg's head off with a knife. Other "execution" videos followed, including some from other insurgent groups, and Zarqawi featured personally in another video in September, beheading another American civilian, Eugene Armstrong. This type of killing is a propaganda technique that is now closely associated with ISIS, but its parent organizations have actually been using it for a full decade already.

In the meantime, the spectre of a unified and secular Sunni-Shia resistance front emerging from the April fighting in Fallujah and the Shia holy cities finally made possible a merger between al Qaeda and Zarqawi's Organization for Monotheism and Jihad. Osama bin Laden, despite his reservations about Zarqawi's enthusiasm for killing the "wrong" kind of Muslims, had to recognize that the latter had been tactically right to reject even a short-term Sunni-Shia insurgent alliance in Iraq, for it was all too likely to end up as a mere nationalist movement rather than a vehicle for the fulfillment of the divine will. In October 2004, therefore, bin Laden bestowed the new name of "Al Qaeda in the Land of the Two Rivers" ("al Qaeda in Iraq" or AQI for short) on Zarqawi's organization, while Zarqawi pledged allegiance to bin Laden. He got the better end of the deal, gaining the prestige of al Qaeda's name while giving up no real power in return.

Zarqawi was unable to stamp out the nascent collaboration between Sunni insurgents and Moqtada al Sadr's Shia militiamen at once. When the city of Fallujah was besieged by American troops for a second time in October, and ultimately reduced to rubble, the Shia militiamen (who were themselves besieged in the holy cities for a second time) sent aid to the Sunni fighters. But al Qaeda in Iraq now embarked on a relentless series of suicide bomb attacks on Shia civilians that gradually extinguished the cooperative spirit and led to revenge attacks on Sunni targets by rogue Shia groups. Indeed, it's likely that by the end of his career (he was killed in 2006) Zarqawi had come to see a Sunni-Shia civil war in Iraq as a desirable goal in its own right, even though it would have catastrophic consequences for Iraqi Sunnis.

Iraqi Sunnis were outnumbered three-to-one by their Shia fellow-countrymen, and would surely lose a sectarian civil war. Moreover, they would probably be "cleansed" out of all the mixed neighbourhoods in Baghdad where they lived alongside or near Shias, and a large minority of the five-million-strong Sunni community would probably end up as refugees, either internally displaced within Iraq or living on international charity somewhere beyond its borders. This made the prospect of civil war deeply unappealing to the average Sunni Iraqi, but Zarqawi wasn't an Iraqi nor was he your average Sunni. He was not interested in creating a good future for Sunnis living alongside Shias within the existing state of Iraq. His first objective, like bin Laden's, was to recreate the Sunni caliphate that had existed in the Islamic Golden Age, and there wouldn't be any room in it for Shias anyway. (Zarqawi, unlike bin

Laden, also had some literally apocalyptic longer-term goals, but that discussion can be left until later.)

If refounding the Sunni caliphate is the goal, then anything that strengthens the Sunni identity and weakens the Iraqi identity of Sunni Iraqis is a good thing, even if it inflicts untold misery and death on the community that is being manipulated. Just as bin Laden was practising a kind of tough love when he staged the 9/11 attacks in order to bring the wrath of the United States down on innocent Muslims—for that would hasten the Islamist revolutions that were in their ultimate best interest—so Zarqawi's civil war would hurt the Iraqi Sunnis a lot but would ultimately free them from their residual loyalty to the "infidel" Iraqi state and deliver them into the earthly paradise of a real Islamic state. It has been suggested that he just liked killing Shias too much, but the deliberation and persistence of his anti-Shia bombing campaign suggest that he had given the matter some thought.

Zarqawi's greatest setback, therefore, was the American agreement to hold elections in Iraq in 2005. Despite its claimed democratizing mission, the United States had originally sought to avoid early elections—the American proconsul L. Paul Bremer had said before the invasion "We're going to be running a colony almost"—but in a confrontation in 2004 with the senior Shia cleric in Iraq, Grand Ayatollah Ali al Sistani, Bremer had been forced, by the threat of a Shia general strike, to agree to elections. The result, as every Sunni knew in advance, was a National

Assembly and government dominated by the Shia parties, now quite legally in the saddle. The new prime minister, Nouri al Maliki, was a fervently sectarian Shia who had spent twenty-four years in exile under Saddam Hussein, half of it in Iran. The long-term goal of takfiris like Zarqawi was the conversion or elimination of all the Shias and other heretics, but in practical terms the elections made it clear (if it hadn't been before) that Iraq would be a Shia-run country, and that his cherished dream of a Sunni caliphate would require the partition of the country between Sunnis and Shias. So from his point of view a civil war between Sunnis and Shias would be a very good thing.

Moqtada al Sadr stood his Shia militia down in 2005, having gained an assurance that American troops would not operate in the holy cities, but the Sunni insurgent attacks continued throughout the year, causing an average of three American deaths a day. In counterpoint to these regular anti-"Crusader" operations were AQI's occasional big bombs in Shia mosques and other Shia gathering places—and, as the year went on, there was an ominous rise in the number of retaliatory attacks by Shias on Sunnis. Zarqawi's swan song was a huge bomb that destroyed the al-Askari mosque in Samarra in February 2006. The mosque, built in 944, was one of the most important Shia shrines in the world. In the days following its destruction, Shia attacks on Sunni mosques and people, and Sunni counter-attacks, killed at least five hundred people, perhaps as many as a thousand. It was at this point that the new army and police force, now largely Shia in member-ship, began to be seen by Sunnis as just more Shia vigi-lantes, only in uniform. There was no going back after the Samarra bombing: the civil war had arrived at last.

Four months later, in June 2006, Zarqawi himself was killed in a targeted American airstrike while attending a meeting in an isolated "safe house" north of Baqubah. One of his wives and their child died with him. According to an American military intelligence estimate, Zarqawi never had more than three hundred fighters, most of whom were not Iraqis, but he single-handedly managed to tip the bal-ance in favour of a full-scale Sunni-Shia civil war in Iraq before he died.

CHAPTER 5

JIHAD: THE IRAQI PHASE, 2006–2010

They say the killings and kidnappings are being carried out by men in police uniforms and with police vehicles, but everybody in Baghdad knows the killers and kidnappers are real policemen.

Iraqi Foreign Minister Hoshyar Zebari, summer 2006[18]

The civil war that Abu Musab al Zarqawi had been trying to start with his relentless attacks on Shias was already getting underway in mid-2005, but the bombing of the al-Askariya mosque in February 2006 gave it wings. The police and various Shia militias in Baghdad attacked at least two dozen Sunni mosques in the city with heavy machine guns and rocket-propelled grenades, and the ethnic cleansing (more properly sectarian cleansing) of mixed neighbourhoods, already a noticeable phenomenon in 2005, gained an unstoppable momentum. It was not that Iraqis were all religious fanatics. There were gradations of piety across the communities, with the Shia the most devout and the Kurds the most secular, but Iraq in general had been one of the most secular countries in the Arab world for a long time.

The sectarian civil war had been deliberately caused by

Sunni fanatics for a mixture of religious and strategic reasons, but the people being pulled out of their cars at roadblocks and tortured and murdered for being "Sunni" or "Shia" were not necessarily religious at all. It had quickly become a war about the numbers, the power and the will of rival communities that had been defined by their ancestral religious affiliations, not about what particular individuals believed or did not believe. Iraqi ID cards did not give the holder's religion, but a license plate from the wrong province on your car or a given name that was identifiably Sunni or Shia could be enough to get you killed. And the majority of the people being killed were Sunni, because the great majority of those in the new police force and the new army, both rebuilt from scratch in the past few years, were Shia.

The death toll was highest around Baghdad, which had the highest number of mixed neighbourhoods. By mid-2006, a hundred bodies a day were being found in sewers or on garbage heaps in the capital alone, many bearing signs of severe torture, including broken bones, missing eyes, missing teeth, burns caused by acid or flame, and wounds caused by power drills and nails. Some died of these tortures; the rest were finished off with a bullet to the head. And of course for every corpse, more than a dozen other people moved from their own homes to some other place where they would be surrounded only by members of their own sect. Three thousand deaths a month, but fifty thousand refugees a month, some moving to a safer location in Baghdad or elsewhere in Iraq, others fleeing the country entirely.

So many were moving that a major study by Dr. John Agnew, distinguished professor of geography at the University of California, Los Angeles, was able to track the progress of the cleansing by satellite photographs that measured the brightness at night of different parts of Baghdad. The areas that had always been exclusively Sunni or Shia remained at a constant brightness (during the few hours when electricity was available) throughout the period, while the much larger mixed areas grew darker as the losing group was killed or driven out, leaving nobody at home to turn on the lights.

By mid-2007, the mixed areas had lost, on average, half their brightness, and the Shias had conquered three-quarters of Baghdad. About half of the "cleansed" refugees—1.8 million, by a 2007 estimate of the U.N. High Commission for Refugees—were still somewhere in Iraq, but 2 million had fled abroad, the wealthier ones mostly to Syria, the poor to Jordan. The exiles included more than half of Iraq's doctors and other skilled professionals, and at least half of its smaller minority groups—Christians, Jews, Yazidis, Mandaeans, Palestinians and Turkmen—who had no safe neighbourhoods to move to. Collectively, they once made up 10 percent of the country's population, but most of them will never return home again: communities with several thousand years of history in Iraq were scattered to the winds in 2005–2007, never to come together again.

This ghastly civil war gradually drew to a close for four reasons: the "surge" in American troop numbers in Iraq; the simple fact that by mid-2007 there were almost no mixed neighbourhoods left to cleanse in Baghdad; an internal power struggle in al Qaeda in Iraq; and the so-called "Awakening" in Anbar province, the huge Sunni-populated province stretching from western Baghdad to the western border with Jordan.

Much has been made of the "surge" in American troops in Iraq in 2007. After four years during which the total number of U.S. troops in Iraq never deviated far from 140,000, President Bush declared in January 2007 that he would send an extra twenty thousand American troops to Iraq on a temporary basis, mainly to help the Iraqi government re-establish control over the capital. In the end, almost forty thousand were sent, and a lot of the U.S. troops already in the country had their tours of duty extended in order to provide more manpower for this job. It seemed to work, in the sense that sectarian killings in the Baghdad region—80 percent of the deaths in the civil war occurred within 30 miles (50 kilometres) of the capital—fell precipitously during 2007. But they were bound to fall anyway, since the sectarian cleansing was a finite task that was an accomplished and irreversible fact by the end of that year.

There is no doubt that the sheer number of additional American troops deployed in Baghdad made some difference, especially since they were deliberately dispersed throughout the city and stayed long enough in one area to get to know it a bit. However, since they lacked the language skills and local knowledge even to identify Sunnis or Shias at any given checkpoint, it seems unlikely that they were the decisive factor in ending a civil war that was fought mainly by means of thousands of individual kidnappings and murders. They arrived rather late in the game, and Professor Agnew's nighttime satellite data suggested that the surge had "no observable effect, except insofar that it has helped to provide a seal of approval for the process of ethno-sectarian neighbourhood homogenization that is now largely achieved." In other words, the U.S. troops simply erected concrete walls, Belfast-style, between the now thoroughly cleansed and homogenous Sunni and Shia areas.

After the death of Abu Musab al Zarqawi in 2006, al Qaeda in Iraq fell on hard times. A successor was announced, an Egyptian jihadi named Abu Ayyub al Masri. Aware that the organization's existing name made it sound like a foreign force in Iraq (which it indeed was at this point), Masri declared the creation of a front organization called the "Islamic State of Iraq" in October 2006, and chose as its leader an Iraqi called Abu Omar al Baghdadi (not to be confused with the Baghdadi who currently rules the much larger entity that is simply called Islamic State). The territory where the Islamic State of Iraq (ISI) had a significant presence and claimed to be in control (although it often wasn't) included the governorates of Baghdad, Anbar,

Diyala, Kirkuk, Salaheddin, Nineveh and parts of Babel and Wasit: that is, the parts of central and western Iraq where most Sunni Arabs live. From that time on, Masri, as an Egyptian, was only the minister of war of ISI, formally subordinate to its Iraqi leader, Abu Omar al Baghdadi—but it was the AQI cadres who still ran almost everything.

This step was exactly what you would expect from an organization whose declared goal was the re-establishment of the historic eighth-century caliphate based in Baghdad, and it certainly made sense to give the organization an Iraqi face, but the Islamic State of Iraq never had any real substance. What crippled it was the rise of the "Awakening" movement among the Sunni Arabs of Anbar province. Al Qaeda in Iraq and its local supporters had established almost complete control over Anbar by 2005, but it had also made itself very unpopular. Ordinary Sunnis in Anbar may not have understood that the sectarian cleansing of Sunnis in Baghdad, just to the east of them, was the direct and intended consequence of AQI's terrorist campaign against Shia mosques and neighbourhoods, but they did see AQI members extorting money, muscling in on traditional smuggling routes, demanding wives from the local tribes, imposing their own extreme version of Shari'ah law—and killing anybody who resisted or complained. There was a substantial reservoir of resentment against them, and American money and tactical support turned it into an actual military campaign.

The Sunni tribal leaders in Anbar province knew exactly

who was to blame for the catastrophe that was engulfing their community: the Islamists, who had got the sectarian civil war going, quite deliberately, with their anti-Shia terrorism. They also knew where they lived. Beginning in 2005, some of these traditional leaders began to collaborate with the local American forces against al Qaeda in Iraq, and other Islamist groups. The American authorities spotted the trend and began working to extend it to other Sunni-majority areas where the Islamists had a big presence. Ex-Ba'athist army officers who had previously fought in the anti-American insurgency changed sides, and tens of thousands of young Sunni men desperate for employment enlisted in the irregular forces that began to be called the "Sons of Iraq." They were paid well (by Iraqi standards) for their work: at one stage 130,000 fighters, many of them former insurgents, were being paid $300 each a month to kill or expel the jihadis. The movement as a whole was dubbed "The Awakening," and it waged an ultimately successful campaign in Anbar and in the "Sunni Belt" of towns that surround Baghdad against the mostly foreign-born Islamist fighters of al Qaeda in Iraq.

> *They hunted al-Qaeda down with a vengeance. They dragged al-Qaeda guys through streets behind cars ... they had videos of feet on the altars in mosques ... It was pretty much just a ruthless slaughter.*
>
> David Matsuda, an anthropologist
> "embedded" with the U.S. army in Iraq[19]

At the end of 2008 al Qaeda leaders admitted that their forces throughout Iraq had suffered 70 percent casualties in the course of the year, falling from 12,000 to 3,500. The loss of influence by al Qaeda in Iraq in these years is reflected in the fact that the U.S. government, having originally posted a bounty of $25 million for the death or capture of Masri, reduced it in 2008 to only $100,000. By 2010 both Anbar and the "Sunni Belt" of towns around Baghdad were largely under the control of the Awakening forces and their American allies. The American forces were also getting a much better flow of intelligence, and in April of that year both Abu Ayyub al Masri and Abu Omar al Baghdadi were tracked to a safe house near Tikrit. It was attacked in a U.S.-led raid, and both men detonated their suicide vests to avoid capture. Al Qaeda in Iraq was leaderless once more.

The steep fall in the sectarian murder rate in Baghdad and the imposition of a precarious peace in Anbar created a window of opportunity for the U.S. forces to get out of Iraq while leaving behind what appeared to be a pacified country with some hope for the future. (Plenty of money was still coming in from Iraq's oil exports, after all, even if the bulk of it was stolen by government ministers, civil servants, and military and police commanders.) Nothing had been permanently resolved, but in November 2008 President Bush, desperate to paint his worst blunder with a veneer of success before leaving office, signed an agreement with Prime Minister Maliki that set the end of 2011 as the deadline for the final withdrawal of all American troops. American combat troops would have to leave Iraqi cities and towns and withdraw to their bases by the end of June 2009. And when Barack Obama became president in early 2009, he moved the deadline for the final departure of U.S. troops forward to May 2010.

———————•———————

So, then, it wasn't all that bad, was it? A total of 4,425 U.S. troops killed (and another 318 dead from other "coalition" countries). At least 178,000 Iraqis whose deaths by violence are well documented, but upwards of half a million total "excess" Iraqi deaths including those who died of war-related causes like the collapse of the Iraqi healthcare system, according to the *Lancet* survey and the *Opinion Research Business* survey.[20] A big butcher's bill, but some people would argue that it was worth it if Iraq finally emerged from its ordeal as a peaceful, united, democratic country. If only.

What had actually emerged in Iraq by 2010 was a tripartite division of the country between Kurds, Shia Arabs and Sunni Arabs. In the case of the Kurds, they received formal recognition in the 2005 federal constitution, which made provision for "the region of Kurdistan, along with its existing authorities, as a federal region" and stipulated that the laws passed and decisions made by the Kurdistan Regional Government (KRG) since 1992 would remain in force.

(The KRG had been created at that time by a Kurdish uprising against Saddam Hussein's regime after his defeat in the first Gulf War, and had been protected until the American invasion of 2003 by a "no-fly zone" that enabled it to defy the legal authority of Baghdad and to function virtually as an independent state.) While the Kurdish proto-state never declared formal independence because of strong opposition from Turkey, which has a large Kurdish population in the southeastern provinces adjacent to Iraqi Kurdistan, its de facto independence continued after 2003.

The KRG's army, the Peshmerga, was never integrated into the new Iraqi army, which had no presence on its territory, and Kurdistan's 8 million people remained largely immune to the post-2003 violence and terrorism that reigned in the Arab-majority parts of the country. Beyond the three governorates that are legally part of the KRG, it maintains claims to other neighbouring territories that were historically Kurdish-majority, including the important oil region around the city of Kirkuk, where a large Arab population was settled during the decades of the Saddam Hussein regime. Most Kurds are Sunni, with a Shia minority, but there have been no clashes between them in the territory of the KRG. For most practical purposes, it is a separate country from Iraq.

The situation was much more complex in Arab Iraq, where about three-quarters of the population is Shia. Having been underdogs governed by the Sunni minority for centuries, the Shias of Iraq were determined to dominate the government that emerged from the 2005 election (which was boycotted by most Sunni Arabs). Nouri al Maliki, the prime minister who emerged after extensive political bargaining in 2006, governed in a relentlessly sectarian style that further alienated Sunni Arabs. His manner was somewhat moderated in his first term by the great influence of the American occupation forces, but after the election of 2009, with the American withdrawal just around the corner, it rapidly became more extreme. In particular, Maliki reneged on a promise to integrate the "Sons of Iraq," the Sunni militias of the Awakening, into the Iraqi army: only 9,000 were accepted into the army, another 30,000 were given jobs in government ministries, and the rest, as many as 90,000 men, were just left out. Shia concerns about the long-term implications of an independent Sunni militia were quite understandable, but Maliki's "solution" to the problem was a blunder as grave in its consequences as L. Paul Bremer's decision to disband the entire Iraqi army from the Saddam Hussein era in 2003. Indeed, the consequences were almost identical: the re-emergence, post-2010, of an armed Sunni resistance to the Shia authorities in Baghdad. Which in turn opened the door for a restoration of the influence of al Qaeda in Iraq in the Sunni areas.

CHAPTER 6

—————•—————

JIHAD: IRAQ AND SYRIA, 2010–2013

The untimely demise of AQI's leader, Abu Ayyub al Masri, and of Abu Omar al Baghdadi, the titular head of the "Islamic State of Iraq," in April 2010 was a turning point for the organization: it was only four years from that nadir of its fortunes to its conquest of most of the Sunni areas of Iraq in the summer of 2014. The person most closely associated with that turnaround is Abu Bakr al Baghdadi, who succeeded to the leadership of the ISI in the following month at the age of thirty-nine. (The name al Qaeda in Iraq was dropped shortly afterwards, and the division between the two organizations, never more than titular, was erased.)

Abu Bakr al Baghdadi grew up in the small city of Samarra, a predominantly Sunni town. According to research done by the *Süddeutsche Zeitung* newspaper and Germany's ARD television channel, he was a mediocre student who had to repeat a year in school because his English was so bad, but he was a very good football player and a pious youth (the children to whom he gave Quran lessons called him "the believer"). He failed to gain admission to the law faculty of the University of Baghdad because of his poor marks, but the Islamic University of Baghdad accepted him into the theology faculty in 1991. He graduated eight years later with a PhD in Islamic theology, and he appears to have passed the remaining four years of Saddam's rule as a junior cleric at a mosque in the Baghdad suburb of Tobchi.

The American invasion in 2003 galvanized him, and he promptly helped to found Jamaat Jaysh Ahl al-Sunnah wal-Jamaah (Army of the Followers of the Sunnah and the Community), a small "army" of militants who began launching attacks on U.S. troops, although, as the head of the Shari'ah committee, Baghdadi probably did not see combat. He was arrested by U.S. forces in February 2004 and imprisoned as a "civilian internee" at Camp Bucca in southern Iraq near the Kuwait border. American intelligence had little or nothing on him, however, and he was not seen as particularly dangerous—just another of the thousands of Iraqi men swept up in various raids and held without charge for looking suspicious. But it was probably his eleven months there that transformed him from an outraged Islamic scholar into a militant and ruthless terrorist leader.

Camp Bucca was a terrorist university. Jihadis who spent time there—and there are thousands of them—still refer to it as "The Academy." Divided into about twenty separate compounds, it held 22,000 people at its peak, including Islamist militants, ex-Ba'athist bureaucrats and army officers who were suspected of being active in the resistance, and many confused people who had no idea why they were there. It was a pressure cooker where new links were forged and new ideas were explored. "We could never have got together like this in Baghdad," said a senior officer in ISIS who was interviewed by Martin Chulov of the *Guardian* in 2014: "It would have been impossibly dangerous. Here, we were not only safe, but we were only a few hundred metres away from the entire al-Qaeda leadership." Not only that, but the same compounds held many former senior Ba'athists, ex-military men and bureaucrats who had been fighting the American invaders in quite separate organizations. An alliance between the two groups would offer many advantages if it could be achieved, for the Ba'athists had precisely the professional military skills and the experience in running large state organizations that the ISI lacked.

Chulov's informant, who used the pseudonym Abu Ahmed, had not known anything about Abu Bakr al Baghdadi before arriving at Camp Bucca, but was impressed by his calm and his charisma. It was the ideal place for Baghdadi to deploy his two most valuable assets—his PhD in Islamic theology and the fact that his family could claim a direct line of descent from the Prophet Muhammad—in order to gain the respect and trust of his fellow prisoners. At the same time, Baghdadi made himself useful to his American captors by mediating in quarrels between rival factions in the camp and keeping matters calm. "He was respected very much by the U.S. army," Abu Ahmed said. "If he wanted to visit people in another camp, he could, but we couldn't. And all the while a new strategy, which he was leading, was rising under their noses, and that was to build the Islamic State. If there was no American prison in Iraq, there would be no Islamic State now. Bucca was a factory. It made us all. It built our ideology."[21]

This new ideology was a radical departure from the ideas of Osama bin Laden and the other leaders of the original al Qaeda organization. Bin Laden was a cautious man who may not have expected to see such a thing as an "Islamic State" come to pass in his lifetime. His plans assumed that he was working for long-term results: first you have to attack the "far enemy" (the Western countries) and get them to invade Muslim countries; that will eventually radicalize the Muslim peoples so much that Islamist revolutions will become possible; and then, even after the revolutions, you have to proceed cautiously towards the ultimate goal of a restored caliphate, always aware that nationalists in every Muslim country will furiously resist being submerged in a pan-Islamic state that would erase their national identities. To use a Marxist analogy, if Osama bin Laden was Lenin, Abu Bakr al Baghdadi was Pol Pot.

What Baghdadi was proposing was the creation of an "Islamic State" right here and now by means of military conquest. It wasn't as rash an idea as it seemed, for two of bin Laden's essential conditions had already been met: the infidel "Crusaders" *had* invaded Iraq, and the Sunnis of Iraq were pretty radicalized already as a result. Keep pushing down the same road for a few more years, be utterly ruthless in using violence to frighten people into submission, and there really could be an Islamic State here and now. It was a tremendously seductive message, delivered by someone far better educated in Islamic theology than most of his audience, and nobody minded that it would all have to be done by force. Practically all the states in the world before the twentieth century had been built by war (and well over 90 percent of them had ultimately been destroyed by war). *Every* traditional Islamic caliphate had been built by conquest, not by sweet persuasion. If you can't stand the heat, get out of the kitchen.

Baghdadi would have known that taking this course would inevitably mean an eventual break with al Qaeda, but he didn't necessarily dwell on that with his audience. He presumably already had the vision of the apocalyptic End Times that would be unleashed by the recreation of the caliphate, which now drives the whole ISIS project, but he wouldn't necessarily have gone deeply into that at Camp Bucca either. What the troops needed was a vision of a glorious victory that could be achieved before they were too old, and—since they were very angry men— theological license to use extreme violence in the service of that goal. Baghdadi gave it to them, and by the time he left Camp Bucca in December 2004 he was a made man.

———————●———————

When Abu Bakr al Baghdadi was released by the U.S. occupation authorities as a "low level prisoner," he immediately joined al Qaeda in Iraq. (Almost every militant who left Camp Bucca carried with him a list of useful contacts to help him rejoin the jihad; most had the telephone numbers written on the elastic of their boxer shorts.) By 2006 he was the general supervisor of the Islamic State of Iraq's Shari'ah committee and a member of the group's senior consultative council. After the death of Zarqawi in mid-2006 he became a senior adviser to the two men who shared the succession, Abu Ayyub al Masri and Abu Omar al Baghdadi, and when they blew themselves up to avoid capture in May 2010 he was elected leader of the ISI by a Shura council (a religious consultative assembly) in Iraq's northern province of Nineveh. Nine of the eleven members voted in favour of Baghdadi.

The organization he inherited was certainly not doing well. It continued to assassinate people and blow things up in crowded places, but it no longer controlled substantial chunks of Iraq territory as it had in 2005–07. Certain things were moving in its favour, however: the American troops were finally pulling out of Iraq; the Maliki government in Baghdad, in its second term after an election in 2009, was more corrupt and incompetent than ever but relentless in its anti-Sunni bias—and elsewhere in the Arab world revolutions were stirring. Not Islamist revolutions, but non-violent democratic revolutions against the sclerotic dictatorships that had ruined their people's lives for so long. The first came in Tunisia in December 2010. Less than two weeks after that revolution succeeded in overthrowing President Zine El Abidine Ben Ali on January 14, 2011 (after twenty-four years in power), the Egyptians came out in the streets against their own dictator, Hosni Mubarak, the last of three generals who had ruled the Arab world's biggest country and cultural capital for an unbroken forty-seven years. Further non-violent protests broke out in Morocco and Jordan (where the kings quickly offered major concessions to protesters), in Yemen, in Bahrain, and—most important for Abu Bakr al Baghdadi—in Syria.

The wonder is that it took so long for non-violent revolutions to come to the Arab world. The phenomenon only started to spread after the Philippine revolution of 1986, but by 2010 it was a quarter-century old and everybody knew (in principle) how to do it. Non-violent revolutions had brought down dictatorships similar to those of the Arab world in Thailand, Bangladesh and South Korea. Non-violent protests very nearly brought down the Chinese Communist dictatorship in 1989, and they did bring down all the Communist regimes of Europe in 1989–91. Others ended almost all of the dictatorships in Latin America, and the apartheid regime in South Africa was forced to negotiate its own retreat from power by the mere threat of one. As a result, for the first time ever, more than half of the world's people lived in more or less democratic countries with free speech, the rule of law, and all the usual appurtenances of democracy. The Arab world was bringing up the tail of the parade, but that was all the more reason why the Arab Spring should have succeeded. Unfortunately, apart from the admirable exception of Tunisia, it did not.

The Egyptian revolution did succeed in removing Mubarak from power, writing a new constitution and holding free elections, but the result, to the dismay of the protesters who had brought about the revolution, was a government dominated by the Muslim Brotherhood. This was hardly surprising, since rural people and the urban poor make up over half of Egypt's voting population. In general they are socially conservative and deeply religious, so most of them would of course vote for the Muslim Brotherhood.

The right strategy for the disappointed Egyptian liberals in the cities would have been to wait four years and then vote out the new president, Mohamed Morsi, for the Brotherhood had accepted a poisoned chalice: the first democratically elected Egyptian government was bound to become extremely unpopular with time, given the parlous state of Egypt's post-revolution economy. They should also have understood that Morsi had to walk a narrow line between respecting Egyptians' constitutional rights and satisfying his own supporters, who expected their votes to translate into a more "Islamic" Egypt. Nothing Morsi was doing was extreme or irreversible, and he was doomed to be a one-term president. So if you don't like it, grit your teeth and wait for the next election. That is how democracy is actually supposed to work, but the heroes of the revolution (or most of them) couldn't wait. They asked the army to get rid of this problem for them, and the army was only too happy to oblige.

Just over a year after Morsi became president, the army arrested him and took over. The military government dealt with the inevitable protests by killing around a thousand Muslim Brotherhood supporters in the streets, a massacre of non-violent protesters comparable in scale to Tiananmen Square in 1989. So now yet another general, Abdel Fattah al Sisi, is running Egypt, although he at least had the tact to hold an election before assuming the presidency. The Egyptians won their revolution, but then they threw their democracy away.

The non-violent protests in Bahrain were ended violently in 2011 by the Saudi Arabian army, which entered the country allegedly at the request of the king, Hamad bin Isa al Khalifa, to put down the demonstrations. Saudi Arabia had no intention of allowing a democratic revolution to occur on an island just off the coast of its own Eastern province. The protests in Yemen were reduced to irrelevance by the spreading civil war in the country. And the protests in Syria turned into a war that has already killed a quarter of a million Syrians and reduced much of the country to rubble.

This overall failure begs for an explanation, since the success rate for non-violent revolutions is generally much higher than that. Erica Chenoweth and Maria J. Stephan, in their remarkable book *Why Civil Resistance Works*,[22] presented a statistical survey of all the violent and non-violent revolutions of the past century, including failed attempts as well as successful ones, and concluded that the success rate for non-violent revolutions in each of the past three decades has been higher than 50 percent (which is far higher, by the way, than the success rate for violent revolutions). One success out of five tries in the Arab Spring therefore seems low, but actually the Egyptian revolution *did* succeed; it was the follow-through that failed. If Egypt were still a genuine democracy today, we would probably count the Arab Spring as a generally positive event, and Syria as the tragic exception. But Syria is the exception that concerns us most, since the Syrian civil war created the opportunity for Abu Bakr al Baghdadi's organization to expand beyond its Iraqi origins and become a phenomenon of real international significance.

———————•———————

Syria, like Iraq until 2003, was ruled by the Ba'ath Party, a party organized along Leninist lines whose original goal was a single Arab socialist nation. The party was founded in Syria in the 1940s, and both its Iraqi and its Syrian wings managed to gain power in their respective countries by the mid-1960s. The two countries never united, however, as the two ruling Ba'ath parties promptly split apart in 1966, and remained hostile ever after. Indeed, the hostility between the two former sister parties was so intense that the Syrian government actually backed Iran in the Iran-Iraq war.

Hafez al Assad, an ex-air force officer, took over the leadership of the Syrian Ba'ath Party in a military coup in 1970, and ruled the country as president until his death in 2000—whereupon the presidency went to his son, Bashar al Assad. But Syria was a very difficult country to rule: Sunni Arabs account for 60 percent of the population, but traditionally for less of the urban population. Other Sunnis, mostly Kurds and Turkmens, make up another 12 percent of the population, but will not necessarily be found on the same side of any given argument as Sunni Arabs. Shia Arabs are 13 percent of the population, a large majority of them being from the Alawite sect (which other Shias tend to see as heretical). Christians are 10 percent of the population, but are divided into many sects, including Antiochian Orthodox, Syriac Orthodox, Catholics of many Eastern varieties, and Protestants. In addition there are 750,000 Druze, plus small numbers of Yazidi, Mandaeans and Baha'i. But all real power was concentrated in the hands of the Alawite minority, some 10 percent of the whole.

This situation had come about because the French colonial authorities, building their own local military units (*troupes spéciales*) in Syria between the First and Second World Wars, had chosen to recruit almost exclusively from the minorities on the grounds that they were more likely to be loyal to the imperial power because they did not wish to be dominated by the Sunni Arab majority. These minorities included Alawites, Christians, Druze and Kurds, but the infantry regiments were almost all Alawite, so when France withdrew from Syria in 1946, Alawites dominated the section of the army most useful for political intervention. It was three Alawite officers who led the 1963 coup that brought the Ba'ath Party to power, and Syria has essentially been ruled by Alawites ever since. Sunni Arabs are often appointed to very senior positions, but the key military, police and intelligence posts have always remained in Alawite hands.

Running a tough dictatorship for half a century gives you time to accumulate quite a lot of enemies, especially if your rule has included episodes like the bloody suppression of the revolt in Hama in 1982. When the Arab Spring reached Syria in 2011, therefore, the Alawites were genuinely afraid that they would suffer severely from revenge-taking if they lost power, and clung to it more fiercely than other Arab regimes facing non-violent protests. Moreover, both Saudi Arabia and Turkey (probably not in coordination with each other) began supplying arms and money to militant groups who would actually fight the Assad regime. At a somewhat later date it is likely that the United States began funnelling weapons into the hands of Syrian rebels from the ample stocks left in Libya after the overthrow of Muammar Gaddafi, although it never publicly admitted it. The net result, at any rate, was that the non-violent tactics which had brought down the

Tunisian and Egyptian dictatorships and so many others elsewhere in the world were never properly tried in Syria, and by October 2011, when the Syrian government first used artillery and air strikes against rebel-held sections of its own cities, the confrontation had turned into a full-scale civil war.

The Syrian regime rapidly lost control of large rural areas where Sunni Arabs made up most of the population. It lost most of Aleppo, the country's biggest city, although it was more successful in holding the rebels around Damascus off in the outer suburbs. But most of the minorities either sided with the regime or stayed neutral, so by early 2012 the military situation had stabilized to a considerable extent, with the government holding most of the major roads and at least part of every provincial capital, but lacking the manpower to take back the rest of the country. At that time most observers still expected that Assad's regime would fall quite soon, but in fact the map has changed little in the succeeding years except for the loss by the government of two provincial capitals, Raqqa in March 2013 and Idlib in March 2015, and the conquest of the easternmost part of the country by ISIS. Which brings us back to the question of Islamic State.

When Abu Bakr al Baghdadi assumed its leadership in May 2010, the group was still called Islamic State in Iraq and it still didn't control any significant swath of territory either in Iraq or elsewhere. There was not much point in launching major attacks in Iraq that might delay the final departure of American troops from the country (by then postponed to December 2011), but the outbreak of the Syrian civil war presented Baghdadi with an unexpected opportunity. In August 2011 he sent Abu Muhammad al Golani, a Syrian-born militant who had been fighting for al Qaeda in Iraq since the early days of the invasion, to create a Syrian branch of ISI.

Golani was a powerful figure in his own right, an alumnus of Camp Bucca who had subsequently been a close associate of Abu Musab al Zarqawi. In 2011 he was serving as the head of ISI operations in Mosul province in northern Iraq. (As an Islamist organization dedicated to the creation of a single globe-spanning Islamic state, ISI has never paid attention to the nationality of its fighters as long as their Islam was of the right sort.) He took some Syrian fighters who had been serving with ISI in Iraq back to Syria with him, accompanied by some individual Iraqi experts. The new Syrian branch announced its existence in January 2012 as the Jabhat al Nusra li Ahli al Sham (The Support Front for the People of Syria)— generally known in English as the Nusra Front—and rapidly grew into one of the largest Islamist organizations among the diverse groups fighting the Assad regime.

Being, like Islamic State in Iraq, an affiliate of al Qaeda, the Nusra Front was placed on the United States' list of foreign terrorist organizations and banned from receiving any American aid. However, it was flush with cash, allegedly coming in part from private donors in Saudi

Arabia and Qatar, and could buy all the weapons it needed (including American weapons) from non-Islamist groups who needed the money. While active in the fight against Assad, it devoted a large part of its time and effort to securing a firm territorial base across northern Syria.

ISI fighters coming from the long war of insurgency in Iraq, whether Syrian or Iraqi by origin, had experience and skills that made them more effective than most of the newly formed, often poorly armed and led militias that jostled for attention in the Syrian insurgency, and so there was a constant drift of Syrian fighters towards the Nusra Front. It was an Islamist organization, of course, holding extreme views on the proper way to interpret the rules of the religion and imposing them on the population within the territory it controlled, but with the whole Syrian insurgent movement becoming steadily more Islamic and less secular in its tone, this extremism did not isolate it politically. Al Nusra grew, it expanded territorially, and it prospered. By 2012, with the Syrian civil war essentially stalemated and the front lines barely moving, al Nusra had grown from around five hundred to about five thousand fighters in a year.

———————•———————

Meanwhile, back in Iraq, things were slowly starting to look up for ISI. The alienation of Sunni Iraqis by the deeply sectarian and staggeringly corrupt government of Nouri al Maliki led eventually to popular protests in Anbar province. Beginning in December 2012, the protests spread rapidly to all the Sunni-majority parts of Iraq, and in the course of the year hundreds of protesters were killed in numerous clashes with the Iraqi army and police. By May 2013 mass-casualty bomb attacks targeting Shia areas of Baghdad resumed after a three-year hiatus (presumably the bombs were ISI doing its bit to help the confrontation grow). By the end of the year Sheik Abdul Malik al Saadi, an influential Sunni cleric, was calling the Maliki government "a sectarian government that wants to smash and eradicate the Sunni people in its own country," and demanding that all Sunni politicians resign from their posts and abstain from the political process. It wasn't exactly a Sunni Arab declaration of independence from Iraq, but it came close. So things were coming along quite nicely for ISI in Iraq, and even better for its al Nusra branch in Syria.

It was probably the brightening prospects for his organization that emboldened Abu Bakr al Baghdadi to take the fateful step in April 2013 of declaring the transformation of ISI into ISIS: the Islamic State of Iraq *and Syria.* (The last word of the title in Arabic is actually "al Sham," a word that denotes not only Syria but also Lebanon and Palestine, but for practical purposes just "Syria" will do. Both the United States and the U.K. governments translate al Sham as "the Levant," a rather antique English term for the entire Arabic-speaking eastern coast of the Mediterranean, and so ISIS is sometimes referred to in those quarters as ISIL.) By adopting the new title "Islamic State of Iraq and Syria" Baghdadi was implicitly folding al Nusra back into the mother organization and downgrading Golani, the leader of al Nusra, to merely the Syrian branch manager of ISIS. He probably foresaw the consequences, but he did it anyway.

> *We inform you that neither the al-Nusra command nor its consultative council, nor its general manager were aware of this announcement. It reached them via the media and if [Baghdadi's] speech is authentic, we were not consulted."*
>
> Statement attributed to Abu Muhammad al Golani, head of al Nusra[23]

Golani predictably rejected the re-merger. There were probably personal and national motives at play here (Golani really was a Syrian, even if his ideology prevented him from saying so), but by now there were real differences between the two organizations as well. The basic religious ideology was the same, but the Nusra Front generally (not always) refrained from mass-casualty terrorist attacks on civilians, and did not engage in the spectacular public acts of extreme cruelty that ISI was making its trademark. Moreover, Golani had the support of al Qaeda in resisting the takeover bid: Ayman al Zawahiri, the Egyptian militant who had taken over as leader of al Qaeda after U.S. Special Forces killed Osama bin Laden in 2010, ruled that the merger should not go ahead. So Baghdadi finally took the inevitable last step and broke relations with al Qaeda: later in April he released an audio message in which he rejected Zawahiri's ruling and insisted that the merger of the two organizations would go ahead. "I have to choose between the rule of God and the rule of Zawahiri," he said, "and I choose the rule of God."[24] A significant number of al Nusra fighters defected to ISIS, heightening the tensions between the two, and the war between ISIS and al Nusra got underway.

You may be wondering, at this point, why we should be lavishing such attention on the tangled political intrigues of organizations that were then (with the exception of al Qaeda) quite obscure. One answer is obvious: because that's how everybody wound up where they are today, and even if you can't remember all the names you get the idea. The other is subtler. ISIS, over the past couple of years, has acquired a vastly overblown reputation as the ultimate "terrorist" juggernaut, sprung from nowhere and led by an evil genius. It is nothing of the sort. Baghdadi is a clever, industrious man who truly believes in what he is doing, but any management expert would recognize that the way these organizations are behaving is well within the bounds of normal business competition. (Except for the particular business they are in, of course.)

The war of words between al Nusra and ISIS in Syria only turned into full-scale war in January 2014, when Golani gave ISIS a five-day ultimatum to accept mediation to end the infighting or be "expelled" from the region. ISIS responded by describing the Nusra Front as the "front of betrayal and treason," and in the heavy fighting of the next four months, *Al Jazeera* reported, the two organizations lost about three thousand fighters killed.[25] A major offensive by al Nusra was defeated, and during the summer of 2014, ISIS drove the rival Islamist organization out of one of its key strongholds in Deir ez-Zor, capturing oil fields that had been an important source of al Nusra's income. That income now went to ISIS, and the group had also consolidated a strong territorial base in eastern Syria, where it no longer faced any serious pressure either from the Assad regime or from rival militant groups. So, naturally, it turned its attention back to Iraq.

CHAPTER 7

———•———

THE CALIPHATE AT LAST!

By December 2013 what amounted to a Sunni insurgency was already underway in Iraq's Anbar province, with the two biggest cities, Fallujah and Ramadi, largely under rebel control. ISIS fighters were visible in many parts of the province and took part in the fighting, but the Sunni resistance was a much broader front in which ISIS was only one element—and besides, at that point the attention of the ISIS high command was still firmly fixed on the war with al Nusra in Syria. ISIS could not afford to fight on two fronts at once, for its total fighting strength in both Iraq and Syria was around seven thousand men. There were plenty of volunteers but they still had to be paid (around $400 a month for foreign fighters, less for locals), and ISIS was having cash-flow problems.

Six months later the situation was very different. The war with al Nusra was over, ISIS controlled eastern Syria (apart from the military airbase outside Deir ez-Zor city) including almost the entire length of the Syrian-Iraqi border, and, now that it had access to oil, its cash flow problems were solved. It was ready to expand both in numbers and in territory, and Iraq was practically begging for its attention. The great ISIS offensive in Iraq began on June 4,

2014, not in Anbar but well to the north in Mosul province—and it is unlikely that the ISIS commanders initially thought of it as "great." It was the usual military thing: keep advancing until you run into serious resistance, and then see if you can break through it. If so, keep going; if not, then the offensive stops there. So they were probably quite surprised when they ended up in possession of the city of Mosul, Iraq's third-biggest, only six days later.

There were no heavy weapons involved on ISIS's side; just the usual pick-up trucks with four or five fighters in the back, and the occasional vehicle-mounted machine-gun. There was virtually no resistance west of Mosul, and on June 6 the ISIS fighters—fifteen hundred at most, but possibly as few as five hundred on the first day of contact—just drove straight into the city, shooting up the two-man checkpoints as they passed them. The Iraqi army garrison outnumbered them at least fifteen to one, but there was no real battle. Some small groups of soldiers or police tried to put up an organized resistance here and there, but they were quickly overwhelmed, and the rest was just mounting chaos and hysteria as terrified soldiers scrambled to get out of the way of the ISIS fighters. Soon they were changing into civilian clothes and trying to get out of the city, for there was no point in surrendering: with ISIS, capture usually meant execution. Hundreds of thousands of civilians also fled east across the Tigris River bridges, including most of the city's Christian, Kurdish and other minority populations. By June 10 the city (pre-war population 1.5 million) was entirely in ISIS's hands. In battle, Napoleon said, the moral is to the physical as three to one; in Mosul it was at least twenty-to-one.

Nobody had foreseen a collapse of the Iraqi army on such a scale, but it should not have been surprising. A small part of the reason was ISIS's carefully cultivated reputation for extreme and bloody cruelty: in Mosul, as elsewhere, they burned, beheaded, hanged or crucified their victims (and made videos when they did these things, of course). The tactic was meant to frighten their enemies, and it did. But the much more important cause of the collapse was the fact that Iraq's army was an army in name only. The soldiers were there to get paid, and didn't always bother to show up between paydays. (This was often a formal arrangement in which the soldiers agreed to surrender half their pay to their officers in return for being allowed to be on permanent leave, and only about a third of the theoretically sixty-thousand-strong garrison of Mosul was actually in the city when ISIS arrived.) Many of the soldiers the army was paying didn't even exist; people talked about "ghost battalions." The officers had paid large bribes to get their jobs, and needed to appropriate some of their soldiers' pay as well as selling off weapons and negotiating large kickbacks on supply contracts in order to make a decent return on their investment. That was the way the Maliki regime ran the whole country: an "institutionalized kleptocracy," as one ex-minister is said to have put it.

Very few officers or men of the post-occupation Iraqi army expected ever to have to fight trained and disciplined opponents, and they were bewildered when they found themselves in that situation. So they fled, leaving behind them in Mosul enough shiny new American weapons to equip tens of thousands of men. ISIS didn't even pause for breath: on the very next day, June 11, its fighters were in Tikrit and the oil refinery town of Baiji, 120 miles (180 kilometres) south of Mosul. On the following day they were only an hour's drive from Baghdad. People began to say aloud what they had been muttering all along: that there were only about five reliable battalions in the whole quarter-million-strong, $25 billion Iraqi army. In that case, the government's only hope was to call on the Shia militias to fill the gap and keep ISIS out of Baghdad, even though that would worsen the sectarian divide. There were about two thousand Iranian Revolutionary Guard soldiers in the country on various training missions, and they were thrown into the breach as well. That effort "saved" Baghdad, but it probably didn't need to be saved: ISIS had conquered almost a third of the country with a few thousand militants, but it would have been insane to commit those troops to battle in a city of 6 million people, most parts of which were by now—thanks to sectarian cleansing—entirely Shia.

Some semblance of a front line therefore stabilized north of Baghdad in the succeeding days—but it did not include the province of Kirkuk, which was occupied by

Kurdish forces on June 11 after the Iraqi 12th Division that garrisoned the province fled south as part of the general rout. Kirkuk was claimed by the Kurds as their historic capital and was a rich prize because of its large oil reserves, but large numbers of Arabs had been settled there—and large numbers of Kurds and Turkmen driven out—as part of Saddam Hussein's strategy for weakening Kurdish resistance to his rule. In post-occupation Iraq Kirkuk remained under the control of the central Iraqi government and not the Kurdistan Regional Government (KRG), but the Kurds were only waiting for a chance to take it back. Owning Kirkuk and its oil would put a firm economic foundation under an independent Kurdistan, so they will not give it back easily.

———————•———————

Within days of the fall of Mosul, IS issued a proclamation about how Muslims should live within the "Islamic State" that had taken them over. (Christians faced three choices: to leave, pay a heavy tax for "protection," or be killed. Shias and non-Muslim religious minorities other than Christians had only two choices, since the tax on Christians did not apply to them.) The rules for Muslims were roughly as follows:

1. People have tried secular rule—now it is time for an Islamic state.

2. Women should dress decently in loose-fitting clothes. They should leave their homes only when necessary.

3. Shrines and graves should be destroyed.

4. Any gathering or the carrying of any flag (apart from the ISIS flag) or the carrying of weapons is forbidden.

5. The police and soldiers of the unbelievers [that is, the Maliki government] can repent. We have opened places for you to do this.

6. No drugs, no cigarettes and no alcohol are permitted.

7. Tribal leaders and sheikhs should not work with the [Maliki] government and become traitors.

8. All Muslims to pray at the mosque at the correct time.

9. The money we have taken from the [Maliki] government is for the public. Only the imam of the Muslims can spend it. Thieves will have their hands cut off. [This rule refers to the estimated half billion dollars that was taken from the banks in Mosul during the conquest.]

10. For those who ask, "Who are you?": We are the soldiers of Islam, and we have taken on the responsibility of re-establishing the Islamic caliphate.[26]

Yet there was no triumphalism, no arrogance in the tone of Abu Muhammad al Adnani, the ISIS spokesperson, when he addressed the fighters who had just overrun much of Iraq in a week: "Be warned and do not fall prey to your vanities and egos. Do not let your egos fall prey to your recent military gains such as the Humvees, helicopters, rifles and military equipment." The spectacular victories were God's work, not theirs. And two weeks later, on June 29, the first day of the holy month of Ramadan, Adnani had a more momentous announcement to make. "The Shura [council] of the Islamic State met and discussed this issue [of the caliphate] ... the Islamic State decided to establish an Islamic caliphate and to designate a caliph for the state of the Muslims. The words 'Iraq' and 'al Sham' have been removed from the name of the Islamic State in official papers and documents." And the caliph would be, of course, "the sheikh, the fighter, the scholar who practices what he preaches, the worshipper, the leader, the warrior, the reviver, descendant from the family of the Prophet, the slave of God"—Abu Bakr al Baghdadi, henceforward to be known as Caliph Ibrahim.

This was not just playing with nomenclature. The last caliphate was abolished more than ninety years ago, when the Turkish nationalist leader Mustafa Kemal Ataturk stripped the last Ottoman sultan of his title—and many Muslims would say that it had ceased to be valid long before that, when it became merely a tool of Ottoman statecraft. Besides, Turkish sultans did not qualify to be caliphs, because none of them were Arabs descended from the tribe of the Prophet Muhammad. By contrast,

Baghdadi's people had put a good deal of effort into ensuring that he met all the qualifications to be caliph: he was Muslim, fully grown, devout, sane and physically intact (a missing limb or eye would disqualify a candidate, because he had to be able to lead the Muslims in battle). And, above all, he hailed from the Quraysh tribe of the Arabian peninsula, or at least he said he did. (It may well have been a tradition in Baghdadi's family to say that this was so, but in practice it is impossible to trace the descent of an Iraqi family of modest standing back fourteen centuries to confirm or reject the claim. And nobody within the reach of ISIS was going to question it publicly.)

Most important of all, Baghdadi actually controlled a state, stretching 500 miles (750 kilometres) from the eastern outskirts of Aleppo in Syria to Ramadi in Iraq. It would have been ridiculous for a group of hunted men like Osama bin Laden and his companions to declare a caliphate. That would have been as farcical as a group of Italian neo-fascists in a *trattoria* somewhere declaring the reestablishment of the Roman Empire. In the interpretation of Islam favoured by the ideologues of ISIS, the caliph must be the ruler of a state, and one that has been in existence for more than a year. That's probably why Baghdadi waited until June 2014 to make his declaration: he had first become the ruler of a substantial tract of territory (in eastern Syria) one year before. But declaring himself caliph was still a breathtaking gamble, because he was demanding the immediate and unquestioning allegiance of all

Muslims. That was sure to annoy a lot of people, some of them very powerful.

"The legality of all emirates, groups, states and organizations becomes null by the expansion of the caliph's authority and the arrival of its troops to their areas," Adnani explained in the statement that declared the caliphate. "Listen to your caliph and obey him. Support your state, which grows every day.... Gather around your caliph, so that you may return as you once were for ages, kings of the earth and knights of war." What this meant was that all existing rulers *and all rival jihadi groups* had to pledge their allegiance to Caliph Ibrahim. If they failed or refused to do so, then they were not just sinners; they were apostates who should be killed. The newly declared Islamic State (IS) was a borderless caliphate that would expand until it covered the Earth (that's why the "Iraq and al Sham" part of the title was dropped), and when IS got to where the apostates were, they would be suitably punished.

This proclamation obviously was not going to go down well with al Qaeda or its Syrian affiliate, the Nusra Front, all of whose members had just been theoretically condemned to death if they did not recognize Abu Bakr al Baghdadi as the one true caliph. The Taliban leader Mullah Omar, Al Qaeda's leader Ayman al Zawahiri, and jihadi ideologues such as Abu Muhammad al Maqdisi and Abu Qatada all rejected Islamic State's declaration of the caliphate as being counterproductive to jihad. The response of Abu Mohammed al Golani, founder and leader of al Nusra, was more concrete. He declared an "Islamic emirate" (one step below the caliphate) in the areas of Syria controlled by al Nusra, with four sub-emirates, two in northwestern Syria around Aleppo and Idlib, and two between Damascus and Syria's southern border with Jordan. There would also be, Golani said, a centrally controlled army that moved between these sub-emirates as required.

What Golani was declaring wasn't technically a state, nor was it formally a caliphate (there can only be one of those), but to stay in the game with Caliph Ibrahim's Islamic State he was edging closer to both concepts. The logical endpoint of this process would be the proclamation by al Nusra of a rival caliphate demanding the loyalty of all Muslims, probably with its capital in the city of Idlib (captured by al Nusra in April 2015 after a long battle) and with Golani as the caliph. It would be a theological scandal, of course, and Golani would be condemned by most Muslims outside Syria even more vigorously than Baghdadi was. It's bad enough to have one fake caliphate; two would be much worse. But the battlefield on which al Nusra is fighting Islamic State (despite the current de facto cease-fire between the two) is in Syria, and proclaiming a caliphate that is not dominated by Iraqis like Baghdadi could have a strong appeal for Islamist-inclined Syrians. One day Golani may decide to go all the way.

————————•————————

The ISIS fighting force in Iraq grew rapidly after its conquests of early June 2014. Willing recruits and tribal allies flocked to its side, seeing it as the only hope for Sunni Arabs, who were under huge pressure from the sectarian Shia government in Baghdad. Islamic State bulldozers destroyed the sand berm that defined the Iraqi-Syrian frontier, symbolically assuring Sunni Iraqis that they were now part of a much bigger Sunni enterprise. ISIS continued to mount offensives in various directions—south from Samarra towards Baghdad, east into Diyala province, west towards the border crossings into Syria, then southeast from Fallujah to cut off Baghdad from the south, switching from one target to the next as soon as their attacks ran out of steam, since it still did not have enough people to push its offensives very hard. Moreover, the resistance was stiffening as the Shia militias largely took the place of the discredited Iraqi army in the front lines. Now it was ISIS volunteers versus Shia volunteers, and it was turning out that the ISIS fighters were not ten feet tall after all. But they were still very good—they easily repelled an Iraqi government attempt to retake Tikrit in mid-July—and in early August they nearly overran Kurdistan.

ISIS troops pushed east out of Mosul towards the Kurdish capital of Irbil, some 60 miles (90 kilometres) away, driving tens of thousands of refugees from the non-Muslim religious minorities who lived on the Nineveh Plains (Assyrian Christians and Yazidis) ahead of them. They struck the Kurdish front line by surprise—the Kurds thought their enemy was still busy further south—and very nearly broke through. Had they done so, they would have been in Irbil in a day. This came as a shock to Iraqis and especially to the Kurds themselves. It had long been believed that the Kurdish army, the Peshmerga, was the most reliable fighting force in the country, but this time considerable numbers of its soldiers were simply abandoning their posts and running away.

The problem was that the Peshmerga's reputation was based on its performance in wars against Iraqi government forces in the 1960s, '70s and '80s. It had not actually fought anybody for twenty-three years, and rapid urbanization in Kurdistan meant that its new recruits were mostly not tough mountain boys but city kids. Moreover, the Kurdish troops were stretched thinly along a front line of 600 miles (1000 kilometres) between ISIS and KRG-controlled territory, and it was not a full-service army with lots of tanks, artillery and the like. The equipment it did have was mostly very old and certainly not comparable to what ISIS had rearmed itself with after capturing Mosul. So ISIS managed to drive a deep bulge into the front and frighten everybody in Irbil half to death—but in the end it did not break through. A large part of the reason is because it was stopped by the first American air strikes of the new war.

President Obama had repeatedly said he would not "allow the United States to be dragged into another war in Iraq" as ISIS swept across western and northwestern Iraq in June 2014. In mid-July he modified this to a pledge that

U.S. military support for Iraq would come only when a new, inclusive government (that is, one not led by Nouri al Maliki) was formed in Baghdad, but it was left unclear whether this military support might ultimately include air strikes or even "boots on the ground." Obama saw getting U.S. troops out of two Middle Eastern wars as one of the most important achievements of his administration, and sending them back was the last thing he wanted to do. But the apparently imminent collapse of the Kurdish defences forced his hand, and on August 8, four F-18 jets from a U.S. aircraft carrier in the Gulf carried out the first U.S. air strikes of the new war, dropping 500-pound laser-guided bombs on ISIS mobile artillery that was firing in support of advancing ISIS forces only half an hour's drive from Irbil. (The planes were coming from a distant aircraft carrier because Turkey had not given permission for its American ally to use the far more convenient airbase at Incirlik for air strikes in Iraq.)

Further strikes followed that same night, and by the end of the month there had been over a hundred American air attacks on ISIS targets in Iraq. There is no doubt that these air strikes were a major morale boost for the Peshmerga, but it's possible that the Kurds could have stopped the ISIS offensive even without American help. They fought well after they got over their surprise, even taking some lost territory back in counter-attacks. In the end the ISIS offensive was stopped and the Kurdish front line was stabilized, although it was much closer to Irbil

(30 miles/45 kilometres) than before, and the important Mosul Dam had fallen into ISIS hands.

What was gradually becoming clearer in this period were the strengths and limitations of ISIS as a military force. Its troops were formidable in the attack thanks to their high motivation and the fact that by now they had considerably more combat experience than most of the forces they fought, but the same tactics that could be used against any other attacker worked against ISIS too. Nor did the ISIS fighters all choose to die where they stood when they were losing; as any other sensible soldiers would do, they retreated. Fighting ISIS is not "a new kind of war." It's just war, that's all.

CHAPTER 8

—————•—————

IN SEARCH OF A STRATEGY

B y the end of August 2014, ISIS's phase of explosive expansion was over, and it now needed to stabilize its control over most of the Sunni-majority regions in Iraq. (For purposes of clarity I will continue to refer to the fighting forces of "Islamic State" as ISIS, reserving the former term for the political entity that controls them.) In the course of the following year Islamic State even lost some ground in Iraq, although claims by the Iraqi and United States governments that it had lost 25–30 percent of its territory were misleading: most of the "lost" territory was empty desert. In Syria ISIS made some modest advances in the north, but was finally defeated by intensive U.S. bombing and stiff resistance by the local Kurdish militia in a four-month siege of the city of Kobanî on the border with Turkey. It had better luck in the centre and south of Syria, achieving a foothold far to the west on the Lebanese border and even seizing control of Yarmouk, a southern suburb of Damascus with a largely Palestinian population, in March 2015. In both cases, however, ISIS troops were actually a small proportion of the rebel forces in the area, and were only able to operate there with the tacit permission of the Nusra Front, their most powerful rival in Syria. (The two Islamist groups had established a de facto ceasefire after their four-month war in 2014 left al Nusra dominant among the rebel forces in the western, heavily populated half of Syria.) By contrast, the capture of the desert city of Palmyra and the adjacent gas fields in mid-May 2015 was an entirely ISIS-run operation.

Islamic State's priority in 2014–15 was not territorial expansion. It was to create all the political, economic and legal institutions of a sovereign state on the land it already controlled and to build up its armed forces. It's not that Abu Bakr al Baghdadi expects to be sending an ambassador to the United States any time soon, or even to be asked to join the World Trade Organization. (A state-owned airline would be nice, though, as at the moment it is still impossible to fly into or out of Islamic State territory on a commercial airline.) At this point the "caliph" and his colleagues are not looking for official recognition from other countries—just as well, since no other government on the planet approves of their new "state"—but they are very concerned to make their regime look credible as a state in the eyes of other Muslims. It doesn't yet have its own currency, but it has released designs for gold, silver and copper coins of the Islamic dinar, allegedly supervised by Baghdadi himself, which will begin to circulate as soon as Islamic State can locate a mint and sufficient precious metals. It claims that a new currency would free Muslims from a world financial order that has "enslaved and impoverished" them, but for the moment it continues to use dollars, euros and Iraqi dinars, mostly acquired by black-market oil sales.

The economy of Islamic State is ramshackle and rather vulnerable. The great majority of its 6–7 million people are farmers and small businessmen who get by much as they did before they were included within its borders, although with drastically reduced access to foreign goods. The money available to pay for the IS government and armed forces is adequate for the moment, but some of the revenue streams that sustain it are unlikely to survive in the longer term. The loot it acquired in the conquest of Mosul—up to $500 million seized from local banks, according to some (probably exaggerated) estimates—was a one-time gain that will not recur unless it manages to capture some other major city; and the substantial flow of cash donations from rich admirers in the Gulf states is in the process of being choked off by Saudi Arabia and other Gulf governments. Its income from ransoms for kidnap victims (an estimated $25 million so far) and from the sale of antiquities that it encourages local residents to dig up in exchange for a substantial chunk of the proceeds ($38 million) will doubtless continue, but that is only a drop in the bucket in relation to its needs.

Islamic State's main cash cow so far has been the sale of black-market oil, mainly to Turkish customers. It is alleged to also be selling oil to the Syrian regime, and some of its enemies seize on this allegation as proof that it is really a tool of Bashar al Assad's regime, created to discredit the "real" revolutionary forces. But Damascus needs oil and Islamic State needs customers, and you don't need a cease-fire to do this kind of deal. Just transfer the money, and IS will send some oil down one of the many surviving pipe-lines. It's just business.

At the end of 2014, depending on whose estimate you believe, the oil was bringing in between $1 million and $4 million a day, but a combination of air strikes on oil wells and storage facilities within Islamic State territory and a crackdown on smuggling on the Turkish border is already cutting into that revenue stream. Which leaves only taxa-tion, and while IS can and does collect taxes of various sorts from the population under its control, they are, for the most part, relatively poor people. It costs a lot of money to run a government that provides even minimal services to its people (basic medical care, garbage collection, clean water, and the like), and a lot more to pay for large armed forces. IS has not solved this problem, and it is unlikely to do so as long as it is confined within its present borders.

How large is its army? ISIS has certainly grown rapidly in numbers since its Iraqi conquests in the summer of 2014. A U.S. Central Intelligence Agency estimate in September of that year calculated that ISIS had between 20,000 and 31,500 fighters, two to three times as many as it had at the start of the year. Another, rather hysterical esti-mate in November 2014 by Fuad Hussein, chief of staff to Kurdish president Massoud Barzani, put ISIS strength at 200,000 fighters or more.

Nobody doubts the fact that young Sunni men have been volunteering for service in ISIS in significant numbers, especially in the recently conquered areas of Iraq where Sunnis live in daily fear of the return of the Baghdad government and its Shia militias. But even if we accept the conclusion of a study by the Iraqi National Security Adviser's office in Baghdad, produced before the events of June 2014, which stated that whenever one hundred (ISIS) jihadis enter a Sunni-majority district of Iraq, they soon recruit five to ten times their number of local volunteers, it is implausible that ISIS has 200,000 men under arms, unless part-time local militias are being included in that total. Full-time volunteers who can be sent wherever they are needed have to be armed, fed and paid. Assume that they are not getting paid the $400 a month that was once the rule for foreigner volunteers but only half that amount; assume also that the monthly cost of feeding, housing, arming and transporting them averages out at only another $100 a head, and the cost of maintaining an army of 200,000 men still works out to $60 million a month. Islamic State does not have that kind of money. A more plausible estimate would be around fifty thousand full-time fighters. That is quite a serious army if they are well trained, highly motivated troops, but it's not exactly the Mongol hordes.

This is the army and state that the Iraqi and Syrian governments, and the United States and all its Western and Arab allies, have decided to take on and (in President

Obama's words) "degrade and ultimately defeat." That is not an impossible task, but it is bound to be a difficult and lengthy one. It will certainly not be accomplished by air power alone.

———————•———————

The idea that the United States or any outside power would perpetually defeat ISIL [i.e., ISIS] I think is unrealistic. . . . We can rout ISIL on the ground and keep a lid on things temporarily, but then as soon as we leave, the same problems come back again. So we've got to make sure that Iraqis understand [that] in the end they are responsible for their own security.

President Barack Obama, press conference, August 28, 2014[27]

President Obama was talking about ISIS forces in Iraq, where the United States had already been carrying out air strikes for three weeks, but as he was about to close the conference one of the reporters called out asking what he planned to do about ISIS in Syria. The two are part of the same Islamic State, after all, and ISIS does not even recognize any border between them. "We don't have a strategy yet," said President Obama, a full three weeks after he authorized American air strikes in Iraq.[28] It was unwise to say this in front of the American media, and they duly punished him for it, but there was a reason why he did not yet have a strategy. It was partly because it was hard to think of a strategy that would have a chance of eradicating

Islamic State without putting U.S. ground troops back into the Middle East, which was thought to be politically impossible in the United States after its experiences there during the past decade. Other Arab states, frightened by the rise of this monster in their midst, are willing to send their aircraft along to do some bombing too, but they are equally reluctant to commit ground troops to the conflict. But there was also the fact that Obama was trapped by his own past commitments.

In normal circumstances, the natural allies of the United States against Islamic State would be the governments of the two sovereign states from which it has seized its territory, Iraq and Syria, but both of these countries are problematic for Obama. The Iraqi government's behaviour under Prime Minister Nouri al Maliki was the direct cause of the Sunni revolt that created the opportunity for Islamic State to overrun much of Iraq, and Washington was determined not to get more deeply involved in Iraq's war until Maliki was removed. Even if he did relinquish power, however, the Iraqi government would have to go on relying on Shia militias for most of its military manpower, and that would continue to frighten Sunnis in Iraq into the arms of Islamic State. Moreover, Baghdad was getting much-needed military help from Iran in the form of air strikes and some ground units, and despite the July 2015 deal to ensure that Iran will not acquire nuclear weapons, the Islamic Republic of Iran remains a major bogeyman in American politics.

Washington's problem with Syria was even harder to deal with. In the first flush of the "Arab Spring" the United States enthusiastically supported the non-violent protests in Syria against Bashar al Assad and perpetual Ba'athist rule. Even as late as 2012, with the civil war already in full spate, the Obama administration expected that Assad would fall quite soon, although there was a growing concern that the Sunni militias fighting to overthrow him were becoming increasingly Islamist. Washington's solution to that was to increase the flow of arms to non-Islamist rebel groups, but that did no good at all. Weapons are a form of currency in a civil war, and a very large proportion of those American weapons eventually ended up in the hands of Islamist groups that had the money to buy them (or, if necessary, the strength to seize them). The Free Syrian Army and other non-Islamist rebel groups were already in seemingly irreversible decline by 2012, but American policy ignored this fact and continued to insist that the only way out of the civil war was the early departure of Assad from power. Indeed, when Syria was accused of using chemical weapons in the war in 2013, the United States went right to the brink of starting a bombing campaign against the Assad regime and the Syrian army.

It has not been satisfactorily proven that the Syrian regime carried out the chemical attacks on civilians that got the world's attention. The rebels had looted many government weapons storage facilities, probably including some that held chemical weapons, so it is at least possible that the initial attacks were actually staged by rebel forces precisely with the intention of blaming them on the Syrian regime and getting the United States to intervene militarily against it. It is, of course, also possible that the Syrian regime was extremely stupid, and used these banned but ineffective weapons on civilians despite the fact that it would bring the U.S. Air Force down on its head. At any rate, the American government concluded that the attacks were Assad's doing, and since President Obama had previously announced that the use of chemical weapons would be a "red line" for the United States, he now felt compelled to carry out his threat to punish those who had crossed it. He was obviously deeply unhappy about having to bomb Syria, however, and in the end the British and the Russians got him off the hook.

In August 2013 the British parliament voted against joining U.S. air strikes against Syria, with thirty members of Prime Minister David Cameron's own Conservative Party switching sides to help defeat the government's motion. This came as a shock in Washington, which had come to expect British troops to follow the American forces unquestioningly into any war that came along. So when the Russians, who had always supported their Syrian ally, suggested that Assad was willing to give up his chemical weapons stockpile entirely if the United States did not start bombing, Obama gratefully accepted the suggestion and withdrew his request to Congress to grant him authority to attack Syria. With Islamic State only two months old at this point, it was already clear that if American air attacks drastically weakened the Syrian army, IS and its al Qaeda–linked rival, the Nusra Front, would be the main beneficiaries and might even take over all of Syria— an outcome that the United States definitely didn't want. On the other hand, Obama's rhetoric about the evil Assad regime during the previous two years made it very awkward for him to simply switch sides. So he resorted to fantasy instead.

Assad duly handed over all his chemical weapons and the equipment to make more of them, thereby allowing Obama to retreat from his "red line" and abstain from bombing the Syrian army. In September 2014, he also extended the U.S. air attacks on Islamic State to include its territory in Syria as well (without asking Damascus's permission, but Assad did not protest). But rather than accept the strategic logic of the situation, which would have required him to back the Assad regime as the sole remaining bulwark against an Islamist takeover of all of Syria, Obama proposed to build up the surviving non-Islamist rebel groups into a "third force" that would be able to both destroy the Islamic State and overthrow the Syrian dictator. Nobody with any knowledge of the reality on the ground believes that this could actually succeed, but the new policy was accepted in official Washington as an essential face-saving measure. (This policy was sarcastically known among Western politicians and diplomats as, "The enemy of my enemy is not necessarily my friend.")

United States policy is almost as muddled in Iraq. Maliki finally resigned as prime minister after eight years of misrule in August 2014 and was succeeded by Haider al Abadi, another Shia Muslim and leader of the Islamic Dawa Party. This changed the optics in Baghdad, for Abadi, who spent twenty years in exile in Britain before returning to Iraq after the American invasion, is a less abrasive character who does not openly flaunt his sectarian loyalty like Maliki. But the rebuilding of the Iraqi army after the disastrous collapse of 2014 will be a lengthy task at best, and perhaps an impossible one, for the Iraqi political system remains riddled with corruption. It is still the Shia militias who bear the brunt of the fighting against Islamic State, and their behaviour still justifies the Sunni terror of being "liberated" by them. When the Sunni city of Tikrit was recaptured from ISIS after a month-long battle in March–April 2015, only three thousand of the fighters on the government's side were from the regular army while twenty thousand were members of various Shia paramilitary organizations commanded, in many cases, by Iranian officers on loan to Iraq. And after the city was finally secured, members of the Shia militias engaged in an orgy of looting and arson. Relatively few Sunni civilians were killed as more than 90 percent of the city's population had fled before the battle, but a number of ISIS prisoners were killed by various means (stabbing, hanging, being thrown from the tops of buildings and the like) before April 4, when the militias were ordered out and order was restored.

The United States refrained from providing air support for the Iraqi government forces in Tikrit almost until the end of the battle, presumably out of unease at the presence of so many Iranian military. It profoundly disapproves of the conduct of the Shia militias, which it knows will make the task of recovering the rest of Iraq much more difficult (if it can be done at all). But these are the allies it has in Iraq, and it will have to live with them or leave.

———————————•———————————

This [Arab] nation, in its darkest hour, has never faced a challenge to its existence and a threat to its identity like the one it's facing now.

General Abdel Fattah al Sisi, president of Egypt as of June 2014[29]

The propaganda about the terrible threat to world order posed by Islamic State (ably assisted by ISIS's policy of frequent and gory "executions" of Western hostages) has been having some effect on American public opinion. By the spring of 2015 opinion polls in the United States were showing that half of the respondents would support sending "limited numbers" of U.S. troops into combat against Islamic State "as part of a coalition." But President Obama clearly has his doubts about the solidity of American public support for a new combat mission in the Middle East. In the request he sent to Congress in February 2015 for formal authority to use military force against Islamic

State, he specifically excluded "enduring offensive ground combat operations" against ISIS by U.S. troops. Gen. Martin Dempsey, chairman of the Joint Chiefs of Staff, told a congressional panel in early March that he would consider using U.S. ground troops against ISIS in Iraq and Syria if necessary, but a spokesman hastily added that his remarks were "hypothetical." There are about three thousand American ground troops in Iraq already, but their role is to train and advise Iraqi troops, not to fight as combat units, and everyone concerned is very conscious of the danger of the "slippery slope" (or, as it is called in military circles, "mission creep").

There is little danger of U.S. ground troops fighting ISIS directly unless a broad coalition of Arab countries is also willing to use force on the ground, and that is very unlikely. The Iraqi and Syrian regimes could certainly cooperate militarily if that helped them in their separate struggles against Sunni Islamist rebels: both are Shia regimes and both are more or less allied to Iran. The problem is that all the other potential members of a grand Arab coalition are Sunni Muslim states that have talked themselves into the paranoid belief that there is an Iranian-led Shia offensive against Sunnis in general. Persuading them to commit ground troops to defend the Shia regimes of Iraq and Syria, even against such a hostile power as Islamic State, would be asking a great deal of American diplomacy.

There was some progress towards the creation of a grand coalition of Sunni Arab states in the early spring of 2015, but it came in the wrong place. To almost everybody's surprise, Saudi Arabia launched air attacks against Shia rebels in Yemen, who it alleged were backed and armed by Iran. This was pure fantasy: the Houthis, a coalition of northern Yemeni tribes, have been prominent military players for decades in the perpetual "Game of Thrones" that is traditional Yemeni tribal politics. They fought off six offensives by the central government in the first decade of this century, and nobody accused them of being Iranian-backed then, even though they are Shias (of the Zaidi persuasion, which exists nowhere but in Yemen). Moreover, Iran is far from Yemen, with no way of sending arms to the Houthis except by easily blockaded sea routes and no plausible strategic reason to want the place anyway. But in the chaos that followed the Saudi-backed removal of Yemen's long-ruling president, Ali Abdullah Saleh, in 2012, the Houthis did very well militarily. They managed to capture the capital, Sanaa, in September 2014, and by the early spring of 2015 they were overrunning the south of the country as well. At the end of March the Saudis declared an emergency and started bombing Houthi forces (and unfortunate civilians who happened to be nearby) all over western Yemen. They also took advantage of the occasion to call a conference of the Arab League and build a new alliance of all the Sunni Arab states.

It was formally a conference to put together an Arab military coalition against the Houthis in Yemen, and almost all the Sunni-ruled states were happy to sign up for that: Saudi Arabia and all the smaller Gulf states (except Oman), Egypt, Tunisia, Morocco, even Sudan. They all promised to send token numbers of aircraft to help Saudi Arabia bomb Yemen, and there was even talk of Egypt, Saudi Arabia and Pakistan (not an Arab state) sending troops into Yemen on the ground. But this ad hoc coalition is also supposed to turn into a permanent joint Arab military force once the general staffs have worked things out, and the obvious and indeed only target of such a pan-Sunni Arab alliance is the evil Shias. But the "evil Shias" include the Shia governments of Iraq and Syria that are fighting Islamic State on the ground. How does this new alliance (assuming it survives) provide the United States with the political cover of an Arab anti-Islamic State coalition that will enable it to commit ground troops to the task itself? Answer: it doesn't.

The truth is that a year after Barack Obama admitted that he didn't yet have a coherent strategy for destroying Islamic State, he still didn't have one. (Indeed, in January 2015 retired U.S. general James Mattis told the Senate Armed Forces Committee exactly that, declaring that the United States policy towards Islamic State is "strategy-free"). The Sunni Arab states have no serious strategy either: none of them will commit ground troops to defend the Shia regimes of Iraq and Syria even from Sunni fanatics as extreme and repellent as those of Islamic State.

What Obama could do, if he were willing to pay the diplomatic price, is to forget all his scruples and help

Bashar al Assad's regime with arms and money, because the Syrian regime is becoming vulnerable to military defeat at the hands of Islamic State and its rivals and fellow Islamists of the Nusra Front. After four years of war the Syrian army is very tired, its manpower is running short, and after some territorial gains from the rebels in 2013–14 it is losing ground again. But the diplomatic price for America would be quite high: the alienation of its Sunni Arab allies and also of Turkey, whose pro-Sunni president, Recep Tayyip Erdoğan, is deeply committed to the over-throw of Assad and has been allowing foreign would-be jihadis to use his country as their easy route into Islamic State. There would also be a moral price to pay, no matter how you want to calculate that.

One cannot help thinking, however, that Obama's dilemma is also his salvation. No matter how hard the hawks in Congress, the American media, and at least some senior officers in the Pentagon (certainly not all of them) press him to commit to another crusade in the Middle East, he simply can't come up with a plausible and defensible strategy for doing so. He should be grateful, because that is really the right answer: don't do it. You'll only encourage them. Hardly a week passes without some Islamic State spokesman wishing that his jihadis could fight American troops directly. And it's not just bravado. It's a rational part of Islamic State's strategy. But it's also an essential part of its ideology. It's all very well murdering Shias and so on, but ISIS needs real infidels to fight.

On November 13, 2014, Islamic State's Al Furqan Media Foundation released a speech by Abu Bakr al Baghdadi entitled (much in the style of papal encyclicals) "Even if the Disbelievers Despise Such," which said in part:

America, Europe, Australia, Canada, (and) their apostate tails and slaves from amongst the rulers of the Muslims' lands were terrified by the Islamic State. . . . The leaders of the Jews, Crusaders, apostates, their devils, chiefs and seniors gathered. They thought, planned, calculated, plotted and schemed for war against the Islamic State. They then came out with a failing plan manifested by bombarding the positions, battalions, vehicles and soldiers of the Islamic State with the purpose of preventing its advance and march. . . . Quickly the failure of their plan became apparent, by Allah's favour. And soon the Jews and Crusaders will be forced to come down to the ground and send their ground forces to their deaths and destruction, by Allah's permission. Rather, in actuality, this has already begun.

Here is Obama who has ordered the deployment of 1,500 additional soldiers under the claim that they are advisers because the Crusaders' airstrikes and constant bombardment—day and night—upon the positions of the Islamic State have not prevented its advance nor weakened its resolve. . . . And indeed, the Crusaders will be defeated. By Allah's permission, they will be defeated. . . . Be assured, O Muslims, for your State is good and in the best condition. Its march will not stop and it will continue to expand, by Allah's permission, even if the disbelievers despise such.[30]

So don't give them what they want. Don't send American ground troops into combat in Iraq, and don't even think of sending them into Syria.

CHAPTER 9

———•———

FOREIGN FIGHTERS
AND FRANCHISE WARS

What really worries people about Islamic State is the possibility that it might expand into territories that would give it a strong economic base, or (at the extreme end of implausibility) even achieve its declared goal of sweeping much or all of the Arab world into its new caliphate. There's not much risk that it will conquer Iraq's Shia-majority region or Kurdistan, now that the first shock of its expansion up to their borders has passed, for both could count on strong Iranian military support if required. Syria is a more worrisome case, for a jihadi victory in Syria would bring Islamic State (and, in the north, perhaps also the Nusra emirate) right up to the borders of Lebanon and northern Israel. Millions more refugees would pour across the borders into Lebanon and Jordan (which have already taken in several million Syrian refugees), possibly with Islamist fighters in hot pursuit. This would create a high probability of a direct military confrontation with Israel, even if the Islamists would really prefer to concentrate on killing Shias first.

But it is the grand strategic ambitions of Islamic State that transfix people, and other Islamist organizations with some actual territory under their control have already pledged their allegiance to Islamic State in Egypt, Libya, Yemen, Nigeria and Afghanistan. There are also lone-wolf terrorists in the West who claim to be acting in the service of Islamic State. How seriously should we take all this?

In the case of terrorist attacks in Western countries, not very. Anybody Islamic State sends out to make attacks in Western countries would have to pass through the same airports and the same security checks that other would-be terrorists have had to go through for years now, so nothing has changed there. In any case, ISIS is far more interested in attracting young Western Muslims to come and fight for Islamic State on home ground. Foreign volunteers are not much use militarily, as they lack the combat experience of their locally born fellow jihadis, and their generally limited command of Arabic makes them unsuited for even junior positions of command, but they make great propaganda. Muhammad Emwazi, known to the British mass media as "Jihadi John," is a good example. Born in Kuwait to Bedouin parents, he grew up in north London and did a degree in Information Systems at the University of Westminster. The videos of him dressed all in black with the obligatory face-mask, speaking English with a London accent as he saws some American or British hostage's head off with a knife, are calculated to cause maximum distress to the average viewer while at the same time being attractive to potential recruits.

Or take the case of André Poulin.

It's actually quite rare for an identifiable soldier, known by name, to be filmed in combat at the moment of his death. It's even rarer to have lots of interview footage of that same soldier talking about why he is fighting and how happy he is to be in the war before he dies. But Abu Muslim al-Kanadi (born André Poulin) got lucky, and all the footage ended up in a recruitment video for ISIS.

Poulin/al-Kanadi grew up in the gold-mining town of Timmins in northern Ontario, a bilingual Canadian of French-Canadian origin, and in the video he tells the ISIS interviewer: "Before Islam, I was like any other regular Canadian. I watched hockey, I went to the cottage in the summer, I liked to fish, I liked sports." He worked as a street cleaner and says he was happy in his life. At nineteen or twenty he converted to Islam, a fairly uncommon event in Timmins—and then he began a rapid slide into extremism.

"He wanted to live in a Muslim environment, so he moved in with a Muslim man here in Timmins—a man who had a common-law spouse and a child," recalled assistant Crown attorney Gerrit Verbeek, who met the young convert in 2009. "Not too long after [Poulin] started living with this guy, he started accusing his host of living an un-Islamic lifestyle, and said he should surround himself with more people of the Muslim faith."[31] Then, when the host discovered that his wife and Poulin were having an affair, the latter moved out, making death threats as he went.

Poulin was arrested and charged with uttering threats, but even before the trial he was arrested again when he confronted his former host with a utility knife. He could have gone to jail, but the former host was reluctant to push for that. "First of all, he was scared for his safety," Verbeek told the *Timmins Daily Press*. "Secondly, [he was thinking], 'Here's a young convert who is going off the rails; perhaps if we are kind to him and give him some guidance, it won't turn out badly.'" So Poulin got off with twelve months' probation—and soon left Timmins for good, next stop Syria.

An ordinary story of everyday folk, except for the very last part. Poulin was not a monster, though he clearly had some growing up left to do; he was just another lost young man looking for a cause. (That's probably true of the majority of foreigners fighting for ISIS.) He believed he was fighting for God against people he saw as "infidels," or at least that was how he put it in the video that ISIS shot with him before he went out and died in battle. But he actually died fighting in a turf war between ISIS and the Free Syrian Army: that is, against fellow Sunni Muslims, also in rebellion against the dictatorship of Bashar al Assad, who followed a slightly different version of Islam.

If you know how films are shot and you look at this video, you can't help suspecting that Poulin's death was staged. The video follows him (or at least somebody who could be him—you can't see his face) through his last battle, panning to follow him as if he is a subject of special interest—until he disappears in an explosion. But his corpse, seen later in close-up, looks remarkably undamaged for somebody who has been killed in an explosion. It's not unthinkable that he might have been set up for this, because ISIS generally doesn't see the lives of its foreign volunteers as particularly valuable, because of their lack of combat experience. They tend to be used as mere cannon fodder, or perhaps, in Poulin's case, as raw material for a propaganda video. ISIS commanders would see nothing wrong in this: it serves the cause, and the volunteers were "martyred" and went straight to paradise, so they got what they came for.

There is a good deal of public fretting in the West about what will happen when the Western volunteers who survive their time with ISIS come back to the country of their birth, radicalized by their experiences in the service of the "caliphate," and proceed to wreak havoc at home. But they were already radicalized when they left, probably by material they accessed on the web, or they wouldn't have gone to the Middle East in the first place. And not many of them will be coming home again: they went there to live in Islamic State, not just to fight for it. If they try to leave they will be considered guilty of a form of apostasy and killed, and the few who do make it home will live out their lives under the most stringent form of security surveillance, whether in jail or out of it.

Of those few who return, one or two will no doubt commit terrorist acts anyway—no security system is perfect—but not nearly so many as will be committed by lone-wolf extremists who become radicalized on the web and never go to the Middle East at all. Men like Martin Couture-Rouleau, who ran over and killed a uniformed Canadian soldier in a parking lot in Saint-Jean-sur-Richelieu, Quebec, in October 2014 and was shot dead by police after a high-speed chase; and Michael Zehaf-Bibeau, who two days later killed a soldier standing guard at the National War Memorial in Ottawa and then ran up the hill with his rifle and into the Parliament Building (Prime Minister Stephen Harper hid himself in a cupboard), where he was shot down by the sergeant-at-arms. Both were converts to Islam, both had radicalized themselves on Islamist websites, and neither of them had ever left Canada. ISIS later claimed credit for both attacks, but it is doubtful that either man had ever been in touch with the organization.

The right response to this kind of attack is to do as little as possible. Capture or kill the perpetrators and by all means check for gaps in your security systems, but remember that, as with other crimes like murder or robbery, you cannot predict and stop every terrorist incident. Actually, the success record of preventive action with regard to terrorist attacks is better than that with any other major crime, but once in a while an extremist will get through. It is highly unlikely to be a mass-casualty attack—those things are very rare, partly because the involvement of a number of people makes them easier to spot—but occasional lone-wolf terrorist attacks like these two Canadian cases in 2014 must be seen as just part of the cost of doing business in the twenty-first century.

The Canadian government's actual action, alas, was to change the law to give the security services greater powers at considerable expense to the civil liberties Canadians are otherwise guaranteed. This was a quite typical, although almost entirely irrelevant, official response, chosen because it pleased the public (whose fear had been whipped up by the media's normal tendency to obsess about terrorism) and because it served the purposes of both the government and the security services. It's foolish to ask the police or the secret services, "Do you need more powers?" because they will always say yes: it is in the nature of bureaucracies to seek opportunities to expand their control over their environment, and they will seize on any passing event as a pretext to do so. But when that happens it is not really about terrorism; it's about power. ISIS and its ilk don't care about what Western countries do to mutilate their own civil liberties, except insofar as overreaction helps to alienate Western Muslims and make them easier to recruit.

———————•———————

A more serious development is the rapid expansion of Islamic State's influence in other Muslim countries. In the course of late 2014 and early 2015, five Islamist fighting groups in Egypt, Libya, Yemen, Nigeria and Afghanistan pledged their allegiance to the "caliphate" and at least in theory put themselves under Islamic State's command.

Except for Boko Haram in northern Nigeria, none controlled very much territory, and two, in Yemen and Afghanistan, were recent start-ups that were overshadowed by much more powerful existing groups that were loyal to al Qaeda. Nevertheless, the tendency illustrates how quickly the Islamic State franchise is overtaking its al Qaeda rival: it has even been reported that the senior leadership of al Shabaab, the dominant Islamist group in Somalia, has debated switching the organization's affiliation from al Qaeda to Islamic State.[32]

The benefits of belonging to either franchise are largely intangible. None of the IS affiliates receive any material help from the brand manager of the franchise: the parent organization's geographical and financial isolation forbids it. They doubtless receive exhortations and instructions of a general sort from the caliph from time to time, just as al Qaeda affiliates get from Ayman al Zawahiri, but in both cases the lack of secure real-time communications means that the centre cannot exercise close supervision over the tactics or even the strategy of the affiliates. They are essentially on their own, with nothing more than moral support from head office. Within the jihadi world, however, that is very important, as it is essentially a free market in which potential recruits and donors, especially foreign ones, can choose among a wide variety of Islamist revolutionary outfits.

The differences between al Qaeda and Islamic State are significant, even if they are not all immediately visible to

the naked non-Islamist eye. The most obvious is the fact
that Islamic State has actually proclaimed a caliphate and
demanded the loyalty of all Sunni Muslims, including
members of rival jihadi groups, on pain of being declared
apostates, while al Qaeda has so far abstained from doing
so. Several of al Qaeda's affiliates, most notably al Nusra
in Syria, have declared emirates, but emirates only demand
the loyalty of all Sunni Muslims within the specific territory they control. Interestingly, even the United States
recognizes that there is a distinction between the two:
although it classifies both as "foreign terrorist organizations," it only bombs Islamic State targets in Syria, not al
Nusra assets. (However, it does bomb targets in Syria
belonging to the "Khorasan Group," which it claims is a
specialized al Qaeda group based in al Nusra territory that
plans attacks on Western targets. Al Nusra of course inter-
prets this as attacks on itself, so maybe this is a distinction
without much of a difference.)

There also used to be quite a contrast between the two
organizations in terms of target selection. Al Qaeda was no
respecter of infidel lives, and was a serial perpetrator of
mass-casualty attacks that killed hundreds or thousands,
inevitably including some Muslims (like those who happened to be in the Twin Towers in 2001, say, or in the streets
outside the American embassy in Nairobi in 1998). But it
did not specifically target Muslims, not even Shia Muslims,
except on rare occasions; nor did it engage in gloating
videos of beheadings, crucifixions, burning people alive

and other atrocities. Islamic State, on the other hand, slaughters Shias as a matter of policy, and it kills Sunni Muslims too if they defy its authority or are captured while serving the Syrian or Iraqi governments. Its slickly produced snuff videos are notorious. Until recently there was a clear difference of style, and the would-be jihadi could be guided by his personal taste in these matters.

The erosion of this difference has been rapid since the death of Osama bin Laden in 2011. Ayman al Zawahiri, his successor, has been more tolerant of the killing of Muslims and of spectacular displays of deliberate cruelty, or at least less diligent in restraining the various affiliates from engaging in such behaviour. This change is probably due to the pressure of competition from Islamic State, which has been growing much faster than al Qaeda in recent years. Indeed, IS is now the larger of the two franchises, and is challenging al Qaeda even in its strongholds like Afghanistan and Yemen. It is not possible to prove that the ideological or religious differences between the two contribute to this outcome, but they probably do.

Al Qaeda and Islamic State both follow the austere and deeply conservative Salafi version of Islam, but there is a much stronger "end-times" flavour to the Islam of Islamic State. Al Qaeda under bin Laden's leadership, and even now under Zawahiri, thinks in terms of decades, even centuries of struggle before the world Muslim community can triumph over the many separate states that divide it, institute the rule of the righteous (yes, in the form of a restored caliphate), and return Muslims to their proper position as the leading civilization on the planet. A much longer time may be required before Islam spreads to every corner of the world, and even then the End Times may not follow at once. Al Qaeda's adherents still live in the slow, hard world of history—whereas Islamic State believes that the End Times are upon us now. Indeed, it believes that it can be the force that triggers the sequence of events that, according to the prophecies, will lead directly to the end of the world. So for impressionable young men who want to play a key role in bringing about the end of history, Islamic State is obviously the franchise of choice.

Al Qaeda's other drawback in the competition with Islamic State is that it lacks a strong territorial base in the Arab world: Zawahiri and most of the senior leadership are still living in hiding, mostly in Afghanistan or Pakistan. On the other hand, it has no current pretentions to being the caliphate, which means that candidate franchises are not required to pledge unquestioning loyalty to Zawahiri, and that helps to keep it in the running. The line-up of the two teams, as of the time of writing in mid-2015, is as follows:

For Islamic State:

In Egypt, Ansar Beit al Maqdis (Supporters of the Holy House), based primarily in the northern part of the Sinai peninsula. It launches attacks on the Egyptian army, assassinates Egyptian government officials, bombs pipelines, and occasionally launches rockets from Sinai against Israel. When it pledged allegiance to Abu Bakr al Baghdadi ("Caliph Ibrahim") in November 2014, it was officially renamed Wilayat Sinai (Sinai Province), in accordance with Islamic State policy on the names of member organizations. An allied group, Soldiers of Egypt, based in Cairo, concentrates on killing Egyptian policemen.

In Libya, Islamic State in Libya consists of groups of fighters in the eastern city of Derna who came together to pledge allegiance to Islamic State in October 2014. This is the group that beheaded twenty-one Coptic Christian Egyptians on a beach in 2015, triggering Egyptian air strikes on the city. It is a relatively minor player in the many-sided competition for power in Libya.

In Nigeria, Boko Haram ("Western Education Is Forbidden") is numerically the biggest of Islamic State's affiliates. Its leader, Abubakar Shekau, pledged allegiance to "Caliph Ibrahim" in March 2014, and the group is now formally called Wilayat al Sudan al Gharbi (Province of West Africa). It has 7–10,000 core fighters, and until recently it controlled a large amount of territory in northeastern Nigeria, a mostly Muslim region of the country. Its military successes (which created 1.5 million refugees) were largely due to the extreme corruption and incompetence of the Nigerian army, which was also heavily penetrated by Boko Haram sympathizers. A joint military operation by the Nigerian, Chadian and Cameroonian armed forces, assisted by South African mercenaries, took most of the territory back in March 2015.

In Afghanistan and Pakistan, a breakaway splinter group from the Taliban calling itself the Khorasan Province (Wilayat Khorasan) of Islamic State emerged quite recently and has engaged in firefights with Taliban forces and bombing attacks against the civilian population. It is widely suspected of getting material support from Pakistan's Inter-Services Intelligence (ISI), which can use it as a counter-weight to the Taliban if the latter organization becomes more resistant to the ISI's plans for Afghanistan. Despite its public declaration of allegiance to Islamic State, it is not known whether "Khorasan Province" is in contact with Islamic State headquarters in Syria.

In Yemen, Wilayat Sana'a of Islamic State announced its presence in March 2015 by attacking two Shia mosques in Sana'a. It is very much a start-up organization in a market long dominated by al Qaeda in the Arabian Peninsula, and its growth prospects are poor.

In the Philippines, the leader of Abu Sayyaf, a militant Islamist group in the southwest of the country, was the first foreign jihadi leader to pledge allegiance to Islamic State and its "caliph" in July 2014. It is very unlikely that he gets orders or financial support from IS.

For al Qaeda:

In Syria, the Nusra Front is al Qaeda's biggest and most successful operation. It was acquired from Islamic State in 2013 after its leader in Syria, Abu Muhammad al Golani, broke away rather than allow al Nusra to be reabsorbed by its parent organization, then known as Islamic State in Iraq. Al Nusra controls all of Idlib province in the north-west and much territory in the south between Damascus and the Jordanian border. If the Syrian regime were to collapse, it could provide a territorial base for al Qaeda in western Syria comparable to the one that Islamic State enjoys in eastern Syria and western Iraq.

In Somalia, al Shabaab, the dominant Islamist organization in that country, is al Qaeda's second-biggest franchise. It once controlled most of southern Somalia, but military offensives by a 22,000-man African Union force drawn mainly from Uganda, Kenya and Ethiopia have now substantially reduced its territory. It nevertheless remains capable of carrying out regular terrorist attacks in Somalia's capital, Mogadishu, and also in Kenyan towns and cities.

In Yemen, al Qaeda in the Arabian Peninsula (AQAP) conquered most of the country's eastern provinces in March and April 2015, taking advantage of the war between Houthi rebels who controlled most of western Yemen, the densely populated agricultural heartland of the country, and a Saudi-led coalition that was bombing them. It now controls about half of Yemen's territory, but less than a tenth of its population. Its Saudi Arabian branch has been savagely suppressed. It is now the largest source of terrorist attacks against Western countries, and took credit for the Paris attack on *Charlie Hebdo* in January 2015.

In North Africa, al Qaeda in the Islamic Maghreb (AQIM) is an Algerian-based group descended from the Salafist Group for Preaching and Combat (GSPC), a faction of the Armed Islamic Group, which was the largest and most active Islamist group in Algeria during the civil war of the 1990s. It was subsequently reduced to only about a thousand men by the Algerian government's counter-terror operations, but it has recovered to a degree and was very active in northern Mali in alliance with the Tuareg separatist movement in 2011–12. It has recently expanded into Tunisia and Libya.

It will be clear from these summaries that al Qaeda still has more powerful affiliates but that Islamic State has the momentum. It should also be stressed that other Islamist groups continue to operate outside the franchises. The most powerful Islamist groups in Libya are linked closely to Egypt's Muslim Brotherhood. In Afghanistan, al Qaeda was once closely allied to the Taliban, and links remain today, although the relationship has grown much cooler, but the Taliban were never an affiliate of al Qaeda. Neither were Tehriki-Taliban (the "Pakistani Taliban") nor Lashkar-e-Jhangvi in Pakistan.

The rivalry between al Qaeda and Islamic State has already erupted into open warfare twice: in Syria in the first four months of 2014 and in Yemen in the spring of 2015. While a degree of tactical cooperation persists, further clashes seem likely. The chances are slim that they will overrun the Arab world any time soon. Or indeed ever.

CHAPTER 10

———•———

THE LESSER EVIL

Q: *[Why is Islamic State] not fighting Israel but instead shedding the blood of the sons of Iraq and Syria?*

A: *The greater answer is in the noble Quran, when Allah Almighty speaks about the near enemy. In the majority of verses in the noble Quran, these are the hypocrites, for they pose a greater danger than the original infidels [those who were not born Muslims, like Jews and Christians]. And the answer is found in Abu Bakr al-Sadiq, when he preferred fighting apostates over the conquest of Jerusalem, which was conquered by his successor, Omar al-Khattab.*

Exchange on one of IS's question-and-answer websites[33]

A bu Bakr al Sadiq was the first caliph, ruling from the Prophet Muhammad's death in 632 until his own death in 634, and his main achievement during his short reign was to force the "apostate" Arab tribes to return to the proper practice of Islam. Many of the Arabian tribes that had submitted to Muhammad's armies abandoned the new religion after his death, or at least combined it with elements of their old beliefs, and al Sadiq waged ruthless jihad against the tribes—tens of thousands of Arabs were burned, beheaded, dismembered, or crucified—to force them to return to the fold of orthodox Islam. It was only after these "apostates and hypocrites" had been dealt with that the second caliph, Omar al-Khattab, embarked on the conquest and forcible conversion of the neighbouring non-Muslim peoples. Today's Islamists, therefore, believe they should have the same priorities.

Islamic State leaders almost never use the actual names of the groups of Muslims they want to kill or convert, preferring to use Quranic or historical examples to indicate their targets. There is no doubt, however, that Shias are the primary target: in the same reply on the IS website quoted above, the spokesperson refers to the policy of Saladin, the commander who won Jerusalem back from the Crusaders: "It was said to Salah ad-Din al-Ayubi: 'You fight the Shia and the Fatimids in Egypt and allow the Latin Crusaders to occupy Jerusalem?' And he responded: 'I will not fight the Crusaders while my back is exposed to the Shia.'" In other words, kill the Shias first.

All the Islamist groups share this ancient obsession with the Shias to a greater or lesser extent, but it has been particularly prominent in the chain of jihadi organizations that culminated in Islamic State. Abu Musab al Zarqawi's decision in 2006 to start using suicide bombings to slaughter Iraqi Shias had a specific strategic purpose—to trigger a violent Shia reaction that would drive Iraqi Sunnis into the arms of his organization—but it also conformed to his deeply held belief that Shias should be killed. His successors, down to "Caliph Ibrahim" today, share that belief, and are equally willing to put it into practice.

This is good news, at least in the short term, for Jews, Christians and others who are also on the Islamic State's hit list. If the Assad regime were to fall, however, it would be very bad news for Syrian Alawites and other Shias, who are seen as "apostates" and therefore eligible to be killed if they refuse to convert, and for the Druze, who are seen as pagans. It should be somewhat less bad news for Syrian Christians, since Islam traditionally gives Christians the additional option of accepting the loss of all their political rights and paying a heavy annual tax in order to be allowed to live as a subject people; but Islamic State has killed significant numbers of Christians on grounds that they are part of the "nation of the Cross," which is allegedly at war with Islam. (Unbelievers and those like the Druze who follow religions other than Judaism, Christianity or Islam may be killed or enslaved according to taste.) Hitherto, Islamic State has conquered only areas where non-Sunni Muslims were a very small proportion of the population, and the minorities have been dealt with very harshly. To expect IS to deal in a gentler manner with the very large minorities in the parts of Syria still controlled by the Assad regime would probably be a mistake. When religious fanatics tell you what their beliefs compel them to do, you should probably take them at their word. Millions may be killed.

*Here we are, burying the first American Crusader in Dabiq,
eagerly waiting for the remainder of your armies to arrive.*

Islamic State executioner, speaking on a video of the beheading
of the American aid worker Peter Kassig on November 16, 2014[34]

Islamic State is strictly constrained in what it can and
cannot do by what it believes are traditional Islamic rules
governing the behaviour of the caliph. The caliphate must
not join the United Nations or any international organization, because that would be to recognize an authority
other than God. It must not establish diplomatic relations
with any other country, including other Muslim countries.
(The Taliban regime in Afghanistan in 1996–2001 was
severely criticized by Islamists for exchanging ambassa-
dors with Saudi Arabia, Pakistan and the United Arab
Emirates.) The caliphate may not even recognize permanent international borders of any sort, since all will eventually be swept away by its own expansion. And although
it is not obliged to wage jihad all the time against everybody, temporary peace treaties may last no longer than
ten years (although they are renewable)—and the caliph
must wage jihad against at least one enemy each year.
Islamic State can never be at peace.

The caliphate is even more constrained, however, by its
adherence to what it calls "the Prophetic method" and its
belief that it is living out the prophecies. Early Muslims,

like early Christians before them, were convinced that they were living in the End Times, and that the Day of Judgement would soon be upon them. Contemporary Islamists, wishing to return to the faith as practised by the first three generations of Muslims (*as-Salaf as-Saleh*, the pious predecessors), have restored that "end-times" theme to a central place in their own theology as well. Indeed, they believe they have a script for how the end times will occur, and that they are the divine instrument for making those prophecies come to pass.

This is where Dabiq comes in, for it is where the great battle that sets the End Times in motion will, they believe, take place. It is on the plain outside the town of Dabiq, just north of Aleppo in Syria, that the "army of Rome" will set up camp. (The Byzantine Empire, originally the eastern part of the Roman Empire, was known to the Muslims as "Rum" right down to the fifteenth century. The assumption is that the "Crusader" army that arrives there in the near future will be the army of the United States, the Rome of our time.) The armies of Islam will defeat the Americans and will go on to capture Constantinople, now known as Istanbul—which you might think would give Turkey's president, Recep Tayyip Erdoğan, cause to reconsider his policy of allowing foreign jihadis to cross the border into Syria and join ISIS.

The rest of the prophetic story need not detain us long. It's fairly standard Middle Eastern apocalypse fare: a one-eyed "false messiah" known as Dajjal appears and leads many Muslims astray. He kills the vast majority of the caliphate's fighters, and the survivors, only five thousand strong, retreat to Jerusalem. They are about to be destroyed when the Mahdi, the successor to the Prophet Muhammad, appears, accompanied by Isa, the Islamic version of Jesus. Isa will kill Dajjal with a spear, and the Mahdi will rule over the world for seven years (or nine, or nineteen, depending on the version of the story), bringing peace and justice everywhere. Then, after some further turbulence, comes the end of the world and the Day of Judgement.

All very dramatic, but the only bit that really matters from our point of view is the first bit: the battle at Dabiq that triggers the events of the apocalypse. This is so central to the beliefs of Islamic State that its main propaganda magazine is simply called *Dabiq*. Indeed, this fixation on the End Times was a main source of the dispute between al Qaeda and the various predecessors to Islamic State that finally led to a decisive break between the two organizations. (It is also the principal obstacle today to any reconciliation between the two, their beliefs and goals being otherwise very closely aligned.)

Islamic State has a different strategy than earlier Islamist movements like al Qaeda, but oddly it envisages the same result. Al Qaeda launched terrorist attacks on Western countries to provoke them into sending their armies into the Muslim world, hoping to use those invasions to mobilize the Muslim masses and lead revolutions that would create true Islamic states. Islamic State already is one, at least in its own eyes, and it depends on conquest, not on revolutions, for its expansion.

This difference ought to mean that it does not need to launch major attacks on Western targets, and indeed Islamic State does put other tasks like killing Shias and destroying local Arab regimes higher on its agenda. But the need to fulfill the prophecies means that the "armies of Rome" must show up at Dabiq, and so the West must still be provoked into invading Islamic State. In fact, it must somehow be persuaded to send a large army to Dabiq. That may be quite difficult to arrange, but sooner or later attacks on the West are bound to rise to the top of Islamic State's agenda. So what should the West do about that?

The Western countries face three options: to do a lot, to do a little, or to do nothing. Islamic State's fixation on Dabiq creates a great temptation to do a lot. Why not just put a big Western army into Dabiq? The jihadis would flock there in great numbers, determined to be part of the great victory foretold by prophecy, and they could then be destroyed by Western firepower in the kind of big conventional battle that the West is sure to win. Islamic State would be discredited in the eyes of its own supporters, and everybody else would live happily ever after.

This temptation should be resisted. Why? Even the prospect of such a large army from Western countries arriving in Syria might well force a reconciliation between Islamic State and al Qaeda, which would be a most undesirable outcome. It would also create even greater anger at Western intervention in the Arab world, and it would be practically impossible to just withdraw such an army again after a victory at Dabiq. The pressure to push on and finish the dismantling of Islamic State would be well nigh irresistible, and staying on to complete the job would lead to the kind of military occupation and prolonged anti-guerrilla campaign that the West has shown itself to be very bad at—and neither of its major allies in the region would be willing to help.

Start with Saudi Arabia, for instance. Its relationship with the jihadis has been complicated from the start. Part of its policy, from the Islamist seizure of the Grand Mosque in Mecca in 1979 onwards, has been to encourage and even pay Saudi Islamists to go and live out their extremist fantasies in other Muslim countries rather than practising them at home. That's how thousands of Saudi Arabians ended up as mujahedeen in Afghanistan in the 1980s— and since Saudi financial support was mostly funnelled through private donations in a relatively uncontrolled way, it's quite likely that some Saudi money even helped finance the 9/11 attacks on the United States.[35]

When the non-violent revolutions of the "Arab Spring" spread to Syria in 2011, Saudi Arabia's preferred outcome was not the democratic, secular republic the original protesters wanted. It wanted a sectarian Sunni triumph over the Alawites, Shias, Druze and Christians who make up about a third of the population. So Riyadh and some of the smaller Gulf kingdoms and emirates poured money into the jihadi groups in Syria, and it was precisely those groups that were the first to move to armed insurrection. Saudi money was not the only reason that the non-violent, democratic protests were sabotaged by anti-regime violence (which was then used by the Assad regime to justify savage repression)—but it was probably the biggest reason.

Saudi Arabia's rulers showed little hesitation in supporting the jihadis as long as they were not within their country's own borders. They are, after all, kindred spirits in many ways. All the jihadi movements in Sunni Islam have borrowed much from the Saudi kingdom's own state-supported fundamentalist form of Islam, Wahhabism, including their views on women, their love of antique punishments like beheading, their contempt for democracy, and their visceral hatred for Shias and other minority Islamic sects. It never seemed to occur to the head of Saudi intelligence, Prince Bandar bin Sultan, who was then running the Syrian operation, that what American strategists call "blowback" could affect them too.

Having helped drive Syria into a civil war, Saudi Arabia continued to supply money and arms to various jihadi groups there until March 2014, when Riyadh finally took fright at the monster it had helped create. Bin Sultan was dismissed and replaced by his deputy at the Saudi equivalent of the CIA, Youssef bin Ali al Idrisi. Islamic State, al

Qaeda, the Nusra Front and other jihadi groups were condemned as "terrorist," and Saudi citizens who offered them public support or gave them moral or material aid would thenceforward face long prison terms. It was made a crime for a Saudi citizen to fight in a foreign conflict, and Riyadh called on all other foreign fighters (an estimated seven thousand at that time) to leave Syria as well. "Caliph Ibrahim" of Islamic State responded by calling for ISIS fighters to launch attacks in Saudi Arabia and, despite arrests of hundreds of suspected jihadis in the kingdom, the attacks duly began. Yet the Saudi elite remains firmly committed to the overthrow of the Assad regime at almost any cost, because it will never accept that an Alawite (that is, a Shia) regime closely allied to Iran should continue to control Syria. This means that it will not actively collaborate in the destruction of the Islamist organizations that now dominate the Syrian insurgency, even though the cost of this policy for the Saudi regime could ultimately be very high.

Turkey, the other most influential Muslim member of the motley "coalition" that President Obama cobbled together in late 2014, has until recently been equally determined to see Assad fall. Although a large majority of Turks are Sunni Muslims, it was, and formally still is, a secular and democratic republic. For the past decade, however, Turkey has been governed by the Justice and Development Party, an Islamic and conservative grouping that has finally broken the secularists' long stranglehold on power. Its leader and Turkey's current president, Recep Tayyip Erdoğan, gradually let his religious and specifically Sunni impulses off the leash as he consolidated his hold on power, and when the Syrian civil war broke out he publicly aligned Turkey with the Sunni rebels and against the Assad regime.

In practical terms, Erdoğan's most valuable and indeed almost indispensable contribution to the jihadi cause was to keep Turkey's 500-mile (820-kilometre) border with Syria open. Most of the foreign arms, money and supplies that reached the Syrian rebels came in across that frontier, as did the great majority of the foreign volunteers coming to fight for Islamic State or the Nusra Front. Erdoğan presumably allowed this because he would even rather see Islamic State survive than see Syria's Alawite ruler, Bashar al Assad, stay in power. Since he could not justify the open-border policy to Turkey's allies on those grounds, he simply pretended that he was unable to close it. "We cannot put troops everywhere on the border," is how Prime Minister Ahmet Davutoğlu put it.

This is nonsense. Turkey could station a soldier every ten metres along the full length of its border with Syria, and it would only require a quarter of its army's soldiers (who do not have a great deal else to occupy their time) to do the job. Obviously, that's not exactly how you would actually go about closing the border, but the point is that the manpower to do the job was not a problem—and neither, given Turkey's new status as a major developed country, was the technology you would actually deploy along the border. The border stayed open because Erdoğan wanted it that way.

It's hard to see how a Syria under the control of fanatical Islamists would be to Turkey's advantage, or even to Erdoğan's personal political advantage, and the only thing that their take on Islam and his own have in common is that they are both Sunni Muslim. Nevertheless, *al Jazeera* reported in May 2015 that Turkey and Saudi Arabia had signed a pact two months earlier to coordinate assistance to rebel forces trying to overthrow the Assad regime. The forces to be aided may have excluded Islamic State's troops, but they would certainly have included the Nusra Front's fighters, who now dominate rebel operations in western Syria. But all of this has become quite uncertain after the disappointing outcome for Erdoğan's Justice and Development Party in the June 2015 parliamentary elections in Turkey.

After eleven years as prime minister, Erdoğan chose to run for the presidency in 2014. He was duly elected to this largely ceremonial office—but his intention was to follow that with a constitutional amendment that would turn it into a powerful executive presidency. In the 2015 parliamentary election, quite unexpectedly, his party not only failed to achieve the 60 percent "super-majority" of seats that is required for constitutional amendments; it actually didn't win even half the seats, and will either have to form a coalition or force a new election. Erdoğan seems to have chosen the latter course.

On July 24 Erdoğan's caretaker government announced that its aircraft had attacked ISIS targets in Syria; on July 25 it also began bombing the former separatists of the Kurdistan Workers' Party (PKK) in northern Iraq. It linked the two groups under attack as "terrorists" who threatened the Turkish state, but there were two big differences. One was that ISIS is a genuine terrorist state—though one that Turkey has indirectly aided in the past—whereas the PKK has been engaged in peace talks with Erdoğan for the past two years and observed a ceasefire for the last four. The other was that in the last five days of July Turkey bombed only half a dozen ISIS targets of no great significance, but it hit 186 Kurdish targets with over 400 missions.

A cynical but obvious conclusion would be that Erdoğan is making token attacks on ISIS (and even making Incirlik air base available to "coalition" aircraft, which halves the distance they must travel to ISIS targets) as a sop to the United States, in order to obtain American support for his attacks on the PKK. Moreover, that he is making an essentially unprovoked attack on the Kurdish organization as the key part of his strategy for forcing and winning another election.

Erdoğan lost the June 2015 election mainly because conservative Kurdish voters abandoned his party for a new one that favours reforms that would give Kurds in Turkey full political, social and cultural rights. The only group he might win over to replace them is ultra-nationalist right-wing voters, who were furious at his peace talks with the PKK. So he needed to end his dalliance with the Kurds in a dramatic way, and what better to do it with than bombs? The rest is window-dressing, mainly to keep the United States happy. So long as he is in power, ISIS need not fear a full-scale Turkish attack, and even the Turkish-Syrian border may remain porous.

The only other potential American ally of any military consequence in the region is Iran, which would certainly like to see the destruction of Islamic State, but Iran has no common border with Syria and is not a politically accept-able partner for Washington. It is a de facto ally of the United States in the struggle against Islamic State in Iraq, but it is not a member of the "coalition" because the Saudi Arabians would never permit it (nor would American domestic politics let the Obama administration allow it). On several occasions when the Iraqi army has got into trouble fighting ISIS, only a combination of U.S. air power and Iranian ground troops has been able to save the day, but these two most powerful supporters of the Iraqi gov-ernment will not exchange even time-sensitive informa-tion about incoming air strikes and the like directly. At the insistence of the U.S. government, they only communicate through official Iraqi intermediaries, however long that may take. And in Syria, Iran is Assad's most important ally, while the United States remains pledged to the over-throw of the Syrian regime.

A coalition with divisions and contradictions as deep and complex as these is never going to destroy Islamic

State by a decisive ground offensive, so the United States is quite rightly determined not to commit large numbers of American troops to the task. The option of "doing a lot" does not really exist.

Doing nothing, or at least doing as little as possible, is also a tempting option. It would have been the right choice in almost every "terrorist" crisis of the past fifteen years: Western military interventions have always made things worse. What happens in Syria is not a vital national concern of any Western country. Indeed, what happens in the entire Middle East is of much less importance to the rest of the world than the media and the hawks in Western capitals pretend: the entire region accounts for only 10 percent of the world's population, and only half of the region's population is Arab. In economic terms the Middle East is practically irrelevant, except for its oil. Nor does it really matter to the rest of the world who the leaders of the oil-exporting countries are: no matter who is in charge, they would have to go on selling their oil in order to feed their populations.

On the other hand, doing absolutely nothing might be enough to bring about the fall of the Assad regime and an Islamist takeover of all of Syria, which could mean the death of millions. Preventing that is obviously not a national interest for Western countries, and whether it is a moral obligation or not is a matter of opinion. The West did nothing to interfere with the genocide in Cambodia in 1975–79, and next to nothing to stop the genocide in

Rwanda in 1994. It was very slow in intervening to stop the slow-motion genocide directed against Muslims in former Yugoslavia in the mid-1990s, although it finally did use air power to stop the Serbs after Srebrenica in 1995, and again in Kosovo in 1998–99. So you might say (if you are very cynical) that intervention is a moral obligation for the West if it can be done from the air, without risking the lives of its own troops in ground operations. Which brings us to the third option: doing just a little.

———————•———————

If Hitler invaded Hell I would make at least a favourable reference to the Devil in the House of Commons.

Winston Churchill just after Hitler invaded the Soviet Union, June 21, 1941[36]

You don't get the choices you would like to have; you get the choices that are on the table. Anything the West does to curb the activities of Islamic State in Syria automatically increases the survival chances of the brutal Assad regime. Churchill did not think that Stalin was a good man, and he knew that the Soviet Union was a terrible place. But in mid-1941 Britain was still effectively alone in the struggle against Hitler, and Churchill knew that it needed a powerful ally to win, maybe even just to survive. So he unhesitatingly recommended an alliance with the Soviet Union to his cabinet and to Parliament.

The analogy is not perfect. If Islamic State and/or al Nusra drove Bashar al Assad from power and took over Syria, the West would survive anyway. In fact, it wouldn't even suffer that much damage: this is not an existential issue for the West. But terrible things would happen to Syrian minorities, and with Syria and much of Iraq as a base, the Islamist militants might be able to conquer or subvert other Arab countries, or at least frighten them into silence. These are not desirable outcomes, and if it is possible to avert them at a reasonable cost, then the appropriate course of action to achieve that end should be considered.

The appropriate course of action is to ensure the survival of the Syrian regime. Yes, Assad and his Ba'ath Party have done terrible things (as Stalin did), but they are still preferable to the alternative (as was the survival of the Soviet Union in 1941). The Assad regime's cruelty and tyranny are comparable to Saddam Hussein's record in Iraq but, at least in retrospect, it is clear that it would have been preferable to leave Saddam Hussein in power. Any reasonable observer would agree that Iraq would be a far better place, and that hundreds of thousands of people who died would still be alive, if the United States and its sidekicks had not invaded the country in 2003. The best of the bad options now is to leave Assad in power in Syria, although—horror of horrors!—that would mean the United States was helping a dictator.

It is not at all unthinkable that the United States might help a dictator to survive. It helped Saddam Hussein survive his foolish war against Iran. It backed the Algerian regime in its brutal war against Islamist rebels there in the 1990s. It protected Pol Pot and the remnants of his regime long after the Vietnamese army had ended his reign of terror in Cambodia. It sheltered various South Korean military dictatorships from invasion by North Korea for decades. Some of these decisions were wise and some were not, but there's no principle at stake here. The only relevant question is whether the choice does more good than bad.

———————•———————

At the time of writing, the Obama administration in Washington is trying to dodge this choice by building up a "third force" of Syrian rebels which it hopes will eventually be able to defeat both the Assad regime and the jihadis of Islamic State and al Nusra. However, the "third force" has already been tried, and it failed totally. It was called the Free Syrian Army, and bits and pieces of it still exist on the fringes of the action, but most of its members eventually either went over to the Islamists or sold their weapons and went home. Nevertheless, Washington is still pursuing its fantasy solution, and the first ninety Syrians began training in Jordan under the guidance of U.S. troops in May 2015. The Pentagon forecasts that it will take three years to train and arm around fifteen thousand Syrian rebels in its "third force," which will probably be too little and also too late to influence the outcome.

For diplomatic reasons, since the United States is not at war with Syria, the U.S. Department of Defense insists that these troops will target only Islamic State forces, not the Assad regime. In practice, however, they would likely target Assad's regime as well, since all of Syria's rebels consider it their main enemy, and there would be little that Washington could do about it. But although the "third force" fighters might help bring Assad down, tainted as they are by their American sponsorship, they would be most unlikely to come out on top in the scramble for power that followed his fall. The Islamists would win it. This is a military policy destined to fail, in the service of a political strategy that has already failed, and the United States government would do better to face up to the fact that helping the Syrian regime against its enemies is the least bad of the remaining options.

The least controversial way to help the Syrian regime would be to give it lots of long-term, low-interest credit to buy arms, food, and all the other things it desperately needs. Western sanctions and arms embargoes against the Assad regime could easily be lifted by the same governments that put them in place, and there is no United Nations–backed arms embargo to get in the way: the Russians, who have stood by their Syrian ally from the start, have used their veto on the Security Council four times to block such a thing. But the one thing that might make a decisive difference to the outcome is regular Western air support for the Syrian army, which would necessarily include direct, real-time communications between Syrian ground forces and Western air forces. And we should not imagine that such changes in Western policy would somehow persuade or force the Assad regime to behave a lot better. It is what it is, and more than forty years in power have taught it that ruthlessness is the key to survival.

Would Western military and economic aid without Western "boots on the ground" be enough to guarantee the survival of the Assad regime at this point in the civil war? Nobody knows: in the fourth year of the war, the Syrian army is very tired. It has lost almost half its pre-war strength of 325,000 as a result of deaths, desertions and draft-dodging, but it can also call on National Defence Force militias numbering 80–100,000 men, as well as the help of a large but unknown number of Hezbollah fighters from Lebanon and a smaller but also unknown number of Iranian militiamen. However, after regaining some territory from 2012 to mid-2014, it has begun losing ground again, mainly because most of its opponents are now united under the relatively competent command of the two rival Islamist organizations, Islamic State and the Nusra Front, rather than scattered among dozens of fractious and poorly trained militias.

The Nusra Front and its smaller Islamist allies took Idlib and Jisr al Shugur in the northwest in March 2015, opening a possible route down to the Mediterranean coast and the Alawite heartland. (The Syrian government claims that Turkey helped the insurgents by jamming Syrian army telecommunications.) Islamic State took the Damascus suburb of Yarmouk in April, while the Nusra Front made significant advances in the south near the Jordanian border. In May Islamic State conquered the desert city of Palmyra, which opened the road to Homs—and if Homs fell back under rebel control, Damascus would effectively be cut off from the sea. The Assad regime is certainly in dire trouble: a military collapse in the near future is unlikely, but not unimaginable.

On the other hand, the core of the Syrian army is still intact and quite professional. With better weapons, Western air support, and a boost in morale it would still have a decent chance of reversing the current trend and containing, if not necessarily completely defeating, its Islamist enemies. If you find that distasteful, so be it; but the objective would not really be to help Assad so much as to prevent a genocide and curb the spread of a vile political and religious ideology.

The worst of both worlds would be to wait until the Syrian regime was falling, and then go in to try to save it. That way the West would pay all the costs of intervening in the conflict, and might still get none of the potential benefits.

The United States and a number of other Western and Arab air forces are already bombing targets all over Islamic State, slowly eroding IS's economic base and preventing it from using the fast-moving columns of heavily armed pick-up trucks and Humvees that allowed it to make such rapid conquests in the summer of 2014. Russia and Iran would welcome American military and economic support for the Syrian regime, and China probably would as well. That might be enough to hold the Islamists at bay until.... Until what?

Perhaps until open fighting between Islamic State and the Nusra Front starts up again, or until enough of the less fanatical people involved in the rebellion make their peace with the regime. Or maybe the Assad regime by now is a lost cause; but even so, Western countries would still be no worse off than if they had never tried.

There are no easy solutions to the challenge posed by Islamic State (unless you have a time machine, in which case the solution is to not invade Iraq in 2003). Openly supporting the Assad regime may just be too much for Western governments to bear, or they may quail at the notion of alienating Sunni Arab regimes that are at least notionally Western allies. Even if Islamic State is successfully contained within its present boundaries, there is no guarantee that it will eventually collapse due to internal dissension. But if supporting the Assad regime with money, weapons and air strikes would contain Islamic State and perhaps even contribute to its eventual destruction, it should be tried. A victorious Islamic State, which might well include Jordan and much of Lebanon as well as Syria and western Iraq, would be a major disaster for the Arab world's minorities, an extremely hostile and threatening neighbour for Turkey, Saudi Arabia, Israel and possibly even Egypt, and an uncomfortable if distant presence for everybody else.

We will conquer your Rome, break your crosses, and enslave your women. If we do not reach that time, then our children and grandchildren will reach it, and they will sell your sons as slaves at the slave market.

Abu Muhammad al Adnani, official spokesperson, Islamic State

Don't panic. That's not going to happen.

NOTES

1. "DON'T PANIC" is what it says in large, friendly letters on the cover of *The Hitchhiker's Guide to the Galaxy*, Douglas Adams' masterwork. It is appropriate advice in almost all situations.

2. Senator McCain was quoting from Vince Vance and the Valiants' 1980 parody (during the Iran hostage crisis) of the Beach Boys' 1965 version of the song "Barbara Ann," first recorded by the Regents in 1958. But the only country he ever bombed personally was Vietnam.

3. John Calvert, "'The World is an Undutiful Boy!': Sayyid Qutb's American Experience," *Islam and Christian-Muslim Relations* 11 (1) (2000): 87–103: 98

4. *El Watan*, 21 January 1996, quoted in Michael Willis, *The Islamist Challenge in Algeria: A Political History* (New York: NYU Press, 1997).

5. *The Guardian*, 8 October 2001

6. This document was originally published in *Al-Quds Al-Arabi*, a pan-Arab daily newspaper published in London and subsequently reproduced in English by the newspaper's then editor-in-chief, Abdel Bari Atwan, in *The Secret History of Al Qaeda*, (Oakland: University of California Press, 2006), 211.

7. Original Arabic text published in *Al-Quds Al-Arabi* on 23 February 1998. English translation in Bernard Lewis, "License

to Kill: Usama bin Ladin's Declaration of Jihad," in *Foreign Affairs*, November-December 1998.

8. Richard A. Clarke, *Against All Enemies: Inside America's War on Terror*, (New York, Simon and Schuster, 2004).

9. Teri McConville, "The War on Terrorism: A New Classic in Groupthink," in Richard Holmes and Teri McConville, *Defence Management in Uncertain Times* (London: Frank Cass, 2003) p. 65.

10. www.theguardian.com/books/2009/nov/14/getting-our-way-meyer-review

11. *Congressional Record*, 107th *Congress*, 27 February 2003, House Committee on the Budget.

12. Both men speaking in *Dispatches: Iraq's Missing Billions*, broadcast on Britain's Channel Four on 20 March, 2006.

13. *The Guardian*, 30 June 2003.

14. *The New York Times*, 2 July 2003.

15. *The New York Times*, 22 July 2003.

16. Interview with George Stephanopoulos, ABC's *This Week*, 26 October 2003.

17. *The Guardian*, 5 February 2003.

18. Report by Patrick Cockburn, *The Independent*, 28 November 2006.

19. From an interview with Matsuda by Mark Wilbanks for "How the 'Sons of Iraq' Stabilized Iraq," in *The Middle East Quarterly*, fall 2010.

20. The first study, published in the respected British medical journal *The Lancet* in 2004, estimated 98,000 "excess deaths" (over the normal pre-war death rate) in Iraq in the first eighteen months after the invasion. A follow-study published in *The Lancet* on October 11, 2006 by the same team from Johns

Hopkins University's Bloomberg School of Public Health in Baltimore, MD, and the Department of Community Medicine in the College of Medicine of Al-Mustansiriya University in Baghdad, but involving a much larger sample size and including two more years of the war, estimated that about 650,000 more Iraqis died in the three-year period covered by the survey than would have been expected to die based on the pre-war death rate. It further calculated that 601,000 of those extra deaths were due to violence: gunshot wounds caused 56 percent of the violent deaths, with car bombs and other explosions causing 14 percent, according to the survey results. Of the violent deaths that occurred after the invasion, 31 percent were caused by coalition forces or airstrikes, the respondents said. Both studies were rejected by supporters of the war, but their methodology found about as many defenders as critics in the scientific community.

A further survey published in January 2008 by Opinion Research Business International, an independent polling agency located in London, estimated just over 1 million excess Iraqi deaths down to September 2007, and said that 48 percent died from a gunshot wound, 20 percent from the impact of a car bomb, 9 percent from aerial bombardment, 6 percent as a result of an accident and 6 percent from another blast/ordnance. This report, however, was widely seen as exaggerated and condemned for its shoddy methodology, and its estimate of deaths is almost certainly much too high.

The 2013 study released in the *PLOS Medicine* online journal, while probably not the last word on the subject, was conducted at a time when Iraq had been largely at peace for four years (the civil war sputtered out in late 2007), and interviewers were able to enter areas that had previously been too dangerous. The study estimated a total of around 460,000 excess deaths in Iraq in 2003–2013, almost one-third less than the figure in the second *Lancet* study of 2006. Nevertheless, this falls within the margin of error calculated by the authors of the *Lancet* article despite the much longer period studied in the *PLOS Medicine* survey, since it is well known that violence declined very steeply in Iraq in the latter half of the period. The causes of violent deaths in the *PLOS Medicine* survey were gunshots at 63 percent, followed by car bombs, 12 percent, other explosions, 9 percent, other war injuries, 9 percent, and airstrikes, 7 percent. Those most responsible were Coalition Forces, 35 percent, militias and insurgents, 32 percent, others/unknown, 21 percent, criminals, 11 percent, and Iraqi forces, 1 percent. The argument will never be satisfactorily resolved, but then casualties in wars, and especially in wars where most of the dead are civilian, are never counted accurately: even the deaths in the Second World War are not agreed to the nearest 10 million. It suffices to say, however, that a very large number of people, most of them Iraqi civilians, were killed in the aftermath of the U.S. invasion of 2003.

21. Report about Camp Bucca by Martin Chulov in the *Guardian*, 11 December 2014.
22. Erica Chenoweth and Maria J. Stephan, *Why Civil Resistance Works: The Strategic Logic of Non-Violent Conflict*, (New York: Columbia University Press, 2011).
23. *Agence France Presse* in Beirut, 10 April 2013.
24. *The Washington Post*, 13 May, 2014.
25. *Al Jazeera*, 8 March 2014.

26. These rules, which were posted in public places throughout Mosul, have appeared on the Internet in various translations and even in a somewhat different order. See, for example, AINA News, 14 June 2014.

27. abcnews.go.com/Politics/president-obama-us-degrade-ultimately-defeat-isis-al/story?id=25261946

28. www.whitehouse.gov/the-press-office/2014/08/28/statement-president

29. London *Sunday Times*, 29 March 2015.

30. Translation by Pieter van Ostaeyen on his website Musings on Arabism, Islamicism, History and Current Affairs, pietervanostaeyen.wordpress.com/

31. www.timminspress.com/2014/01/17/crown-recalls-curious-case-of-andre-poulin

32. *Mail & Guardian*, Africa, 26 April, 2015.

33. The exchange is quoted in Jay Sekulow, Jordan Sekulow, Robert W. Ash and David French, *The Rise of ISIS: A Threat We Can't Ignore* (New York, Simon & Schuster, 2015).

34. *BBC News*, 17 November 2014.

35. Twenty-eight pages of *The Final Report of the National Commission on Terrorist Attacks Upon the United States*, which deal with the Saudi role in the 9/11 atrocity, remain redacted more than a dozen years after the event.

36. (p. 106) Churchill's comment to his personal secretary John Colville on 21 June 1941, the evening before Operation Barbarossa, the German invasion of the Soviet Union. https://en.wikiquote.org/wiki/Winston_Churchill

INDEX

GWYNNE DYER has served in the Canadian, British and American navies. He holds a PhD in Middle Eastern history from the University of London, has taught at Sandhurst and served on the Board of Governors of Canada's Royal Military College. Dyer writes a syndicated column that appears in more than 175 newspapers around the world.